Moving On to Key Stage 1

Moving On to Key Stage 1

Improving Transition from the Early Years Foundation Stage

Julie Fisher

Open University Press

Open Univeristy Press
McGraw-Hill Education
McGraw-Hill House
Shoppenhangers Road
Maidenhead
Berkshire
England
SL6 2QL

email: enquiries@openup.co.uk
world wide web www.openup.co.uk

Two Penn Plaza, New York, NY 1021–2289, USA

First published 2010

A catalogue record of this book is available from the British Library

ISBN-13: 978–0–335–23846–0 (pb)   978–0–335–23847–7 (hb)
ISBN-10: 0–335–23846–7 (pb)   0–335–23847–5 (hb)

Library of Congress Cataloging-in-Publication Data
CIP data applied for

Typeset by RefineCatch Limited, Bungay, Suffolk
Printed in the UK by Bell and Bain Ltd, Glasgow

Mixed Sources
Product group from well-managed
forests and other controlled sources
www.fsc.org Cert no. TT-COC-002769
© 1996 Forest Stewardship Council

Fictitious names of companies, products, people, characters and/or data that may be used herein (in case studies or in examples) are not intended to represent any real individual, company, product or event.

To my beloved daughter Sophie

Contents

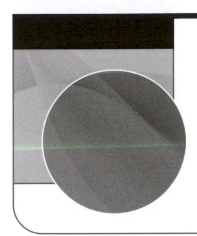

List of figures

Acknowledgements

This book is dedicated to the many Key Stage 1 teachers who have been bold enough to challenge the existing orthodoxies of the Key Stage 1 curriculum and work towards a pedagogy that starts from children and their developmental needs. In particular, I want to acknowledge the contribution of four Oxfordshire teachers who worked with me over three years developing their Year 1 practice and offering me a wonderful sounding board for exploring and refining the messages in this book. So, thank you to Nicola Ball, to Kat Lamb, to Hilary Phelps and to Jodi Stenzhorn – you have been a source of real inspiration. I am also indebted to another Oxfordshire teacher, Jennie Perry, whose outstanding classroom practice I observed some five years ago and who convinced me that developmentally appropriate practice was still possible – and desirable – in Key Stage 1. Also my grateful thanks go to Sue Vermes, headteacher of The Slade Nursery School and Children's Centre, whose wisdom, knowledge and commitment to children ensured that the Oxfordshire research remained true to the highest principles of developmentally appropriate practice. Finally, my thanks also go to Dr Alison Price at Oxford Brookes University who remained so supportive of the Oxfordshire Transition Project and who was prepared to share her considerable skills in shaping and improving our study of transition and of developmentally appropriate practice.

I would like to pay tribute to the local authority lead advisers for the Early Years Foundation Stage who have recognized the importance of transition as an issue within their own authorities and have been prepared to fund training and research to address the issue – even though the teachers they are training are technically not in the 'early years'. In particular, a personal thank you goes to Maggie Smith in Oxfordshire, to Anne Bentley in Sefton and to Sarah Lambert in Blackpool for their support of this work and for their tenacity in bringing the transition messages to their own schools.

I would like to thank Monika Lee, my commissioning editor at Open University Press for giving me such thoughtful and detailed feedback on the early drafts of this book and for ensuring its messages are engaging and unequivocal.

Finally, and as always, my loving thanks go to David, for understanding why writing about these issues remains so important to me, for always being proud of the outcomes of my work and for not interrupting my writing with too many questions, and to Sophie, for interrupting me all the time and reminding me what matters most in life.

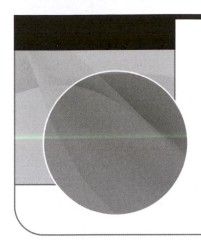

Introduction

This book draws on the development of Key Stage 1 practice in a number of Oxfordshire schools that took part in the Oxfordshire Transition Project (2005–8). The Project lasted three years and involved over 50 practitioners from both the Early Years Foundation Stage (EYFS) and Years 1 and 2. The Project was generously funded by the Esmée Fairbairn Foundation and brought together practitioners working in schools with advisory staff from the local authority (LA) and lecturers from Oxford Brookes University.

The first year of the Project examined the move children make from the Foundation Stage to Year 1. It was in response to the concerns expressed by teachers, children and parents to the sometimes abrupt change from a play-based curriculum to the more formal approaches prevalent in many Year 1 classes at the time. This phase of the Project identified ways in which Reception and Year 1 teachers might work together to make transition from the Foundation Stage and into Year 1 a more seamless experience for all children.

The second and third years of the Project focused on Year 1 practice (and, because some of the classes were Years 1/2, Year 2 practice as well) and involved Key Stage 1 teachers in examining their beliefs about how children learn when they are 5, 6 and 7 years of age, and how classroom practice can be designed to support these preferred ways of learning.

In the third year, four teachers elected to participate in a more intensive analysis of 'developmentally appropriate' practice. They decided that Year 1 teachers were pretty confident about planning for adult-initiated activities but were generally less sure about supporting learning that was initiated by children. So the focus for the third year of the Project became child-initiated learning in Key Stage 1.

The outcomes of the Oxfordshire Project are threaded throughout this book. However, my research into transition and developing more seamless practice between the Early Years Foundation Stage and Key Stage 1 has not drawn solely on practice in Oxfordshire. I have been privileged to work in 17 different LAs where headteachers, teachers and advisory staff have been grappling with improving transition into Key Stage 1, and the messages from these other authorities have served to strengthen my messages about effective practice.

I mention headteachers, in particular, because I believe so strongly that transition is a whole-school issue and that, without the understanding and support of a headteacher, staff struggle to see through the changes to their practice that they may wish to make. Headteachers who are knowledgeable and supportive can not only help to explain and justify any changes in practice to parents and governors, but can ensure that their own senior management teams – many of whom have never taught this age group – do not have inappropriate expectations of children or staff working in Key Stage 1.

One particular issue that is currently inhibiting the improvement of transition in various LAs is that of funding. While those involved with the Early Years Foundation Stage are more than anxious to promote seamless practice into Key Stage 1, their budgets are not earmarked for the training of Year 1 teachers. On the other hand, LA courses for primary teachers rarely, if ever, focus on pedagogy. Almost all primary teacher training is concerned with subjects and, while this might include the 'how' as well as the 'what' of teaching, it is still subject-specific and not generically concerned with child development. Until there is recognition that *how* we teach children has every bit as much impact on outcomes and standards as *what* children are taught, then children's progress will continue to plateau. All teachers need to understand how their children learn best and then have the professional autonomy to introduce that practice into their classrooms.

Finally, it is important to realize that introducing developmentally appropriate practice is not an easy option. It is far easier to sit a whole class on the carpet, teach them the same thing and tick a box as evidence that this aspect of the curriculum has been covered. Teachers will only want to engage with the issues in this book if they recognize that some of the whole-class, prescriptive and didactic ways of teaching that have become prevalent in recent years in English classrooms do not necessarily suit the learning styles of the children they know in their own classes. If you are one of those teachers, then this book is for you.

Please note that I have chosen to use the pronoun 'her' when referring to teachers and other early years practitioners. I have used the pronoun 'he' when referring to the child.

In the quotations from the Oxfordshire Transition Project teachers' logs, I have said 'Year 1 teacher'. Please note that in some instances these teachers were also teachers of Year 2 children but I have not made this explicit in each individual case.

CHAPTER 1

Transition: why is there an issue?

Introduction

Anyone walking into an English primary school over the past decade would be forgiven for thinking that the learning needs of 5- and 6-year-old children in this country are very different. While Reception children are to be found engaged in playful and active learning indoors and outdoors, Year 1 children are frequently found sitting passively on carpets listening to the exposition of their teachers. While Reception children are following their own interests and preoccupations, the 6-year-olds are following careful and detailed planning which is concerned with the teachers' intended outcomes and not their own. Why is this the case? What evidence is there that children in Reception – the year they become 5, need something so palpably different from those in Year 1 – the year they become 6?

The reality is that it is not the needs of children that have driven the wedge between Reception and Year 1 practice, but rather successive government initiatives that have at their heart conflicting beliefs about effective learning and teaching for children who are 5 and 6 years old. In actual fact, it is my belief that government minsters have not particularly thought about the needs of Year 1 at all. Successive initiatives introduced into primary schools over recent years have ignored the fact that the way in which children learn in Key Stage 1 is developmentally very different from the way in which they learn in Key Stage 2. There were good reasons why the education system in this country used to separate children in infant and junior schools. Children's ways of learning alter significantly once they reach the start of Key Stage 2 as they become increasingly capable of learning in more abstract and teacher-focused ways. But the 'primary-itization' of English schooling has meant that initiatives suitable for Key Stage 2 are indiscriminately applied to Key Stage 1 without sufficient (or sufficiently knowledgeable) consideration being given to whether they are suitable for younger primary children.

In order to decide what is truly appropriate for learners of this age, it is important to consider what has influenced the very differing practices in Reception and Year 1 classes and then examine this alongside what is known about the learning needs of 5- and 6-year-old children.

The introduction of the Foundation Stage

In 2000, the English government introduced a new 'distinct' phase of education called the 'Foundation Stage', for children age 3 to the end of the Reception year (the year children become 5). The introduction of the Foundation Stage was accompanied by the first national guidance for those teaching this age group. Entitled *Curriculum Guidance for the Foundation Stage* (DfES 2000), this document set out some key principles about the way young children should learn and the role of adults in supporting this learning. It also established goals for learning that most children should achieve by the end of their Reception year.

As well as setting down standards for the quality of the curriculum, the introduction of the Foundation Stage also had an impact on the teachers who were to be responsible for its implementation. Up until this point, Reception class teachers in schools had sometimes felt pulled between a pillar and a post. While being aware that their children were very young and needed learning experiences similar to those in nursery schools and classes, they were often seen as the first class of the 'primary school' and, therefore, expected to introduce more formal and certainly more teacher-directed approaches. But the introduction of the Foundation Stage brought Reception teachers firmly off the fence and established that they were to deliver a play-based curriculum with substantial amounts of child-initiated learning, and that their role was to facilitate and support learning rather than to direct it.

The introduction of the Literacy and Numeracy Strategies

At around the same time that Reception teachers were embracing a more child-centred way of teaching, their Year 1 colleagues were being moved in the opposite direction. In 1998 and 1999, for the first time national guidance was introduced not just about *what* children of primary age should learn (the National Curriculum had established this in 1989) but *how* they should learn it. *The National Literacy Strategy* (DfEE 1998) followed by *The National Numeracy Strategy* (DfEE 1999) documents both laid down a model by which teachers were to teach these two core subjects. The models – the Literacy Hour in the case of the Literacy Strategy, and the Daily Mathematics lesson (45 minutes) – in the case of the Numeracy Strategy, were highly prescriptive and entirely dependent on teacher-initiated learning.

What was significant about the models for the delivery of the Literacy Hour and the Daily Mathematics lesson was that they offered little differentiation between a Year 1 class and a Year 6 class, between children who were (in some cases) just 5 years old, and children who were 11. Strategies that were seen as effective for Key Stage 2 children were assumed to be equally appropriate for Key Stage 1 children, and Year 1 teachers found themselves having to comply with school policies and approaches that were universally applied across the whole primary age range.

So it can be seen that, at a time when teachers of Reception age children were being expected to follow a play-based, learner-centred curriculum, teachers in Year 1 were being expected to introduce a prescriptive, teacher-centred formula for the education of 6-year-olds. It was inevitable, therefore, that as children moved from the early years to the primary phase of their education, the experiences of many would be abruptly different and create problems not just for children, but for their teachers also.

Reasons for reviewing the transition of children from the Foundation Stage to Key Stage 1

While the paragraphs above have identified why there is currently an issue around children's differing experiences as they make the transition from the Foundation Stage to Key Stage 1, it is important now to review the evidence about the impact of these different policy initiatives on children's actual experiences.

The following pages are intended to give you, your senior leadership teams, governors and LAs a strong rationale for reviewing practice around the transition of children from the early years into primary schooling. We begin by looking at government reports about transition at this stage of education. Then we will look at national data from the Foundation Stage Profile outcomes and what this tells us about children's achievements. Next we look at findings from one LA that consulted its children and parents about their experiences of and feelings about transition into Key Stage 1. Finally, we will revisit what is known about child development at this age, and consider whether current practice meets children's developmental needs. If you need to convince anyone – maybe even yourself – that transition is an issue worthy of attention, then the following pages should give you an unequivocal rationale for doing so.

National reports about transition from Foundation Stage to Key Stage 1

During the early years of the millennium, it was not only individual teachers who were identifying a gulf between Reception and Year 1 practice. Nationally, the Office for Standards in Education (Ofsted) were also identifying the issue as its inpectors moved from school to school.

In 2004, Ofsted produced a report entitled *Transition from the Reception Year to Year 1* (Ofsted 2004). Its findings suggested that insufficient consideration was being given to the relationship between the curricula in the Foundation Stage and in Year 1 and that transition to more formal approaches in Year 1 was sometimes too 'abrupt'. In particular, inspectors highlighted that in some schools emphasis was given to the two national strategies at the expense of regular attention to other subjects.

In their recommendations, inspectors gave the following 'Point for Action': 'Schools which admit pupils to the Foundation Stage should ensure that learning experiences in Year 1 build upon the practical approaches and structured play in Year R (reception)' (Ofsted 2004: 3).

This report by Ofsted was swiftly followed by another. Commissioned by the government's Sure Start Unit at the Department for Education and Employment (DfEE) and conducted by researchers from the National Foundation for Educational Research (NFER), *A Study of the Transition from the Foundation Stage to Key Stage 1* (Sanders *et al.* 2005) found similar problems. These researchers identified the biggest challenge to transition being posed by the move from a play-based approach in the Foundation Stage to a more 'structured' curriculum in Key Stage 1. They reported that the introduction of the full Literacy Hour and the Daily Mathematics lesson were identified, by teachers, as challenging because it was difficult to get young children to sit down and listen to the teacher. The children, in turn, were reported as valuing their experiences in Reception and regretting the loss of opportunities to learn through play. Some children were worried by the workload expected in Year 1, found writing difficult and were bored by the requirement to sit and listen to the teacher.

As an antidote to these concerns, the government's National Assessment Agency (NAA) produced a guidance document entitled *Continuing the Learning Journey* (NAA 2005), the purpose of which was 'to support schools and local authorities in working towards improving transition between the foundation stage and key stage 1'. Here, it is recommended that schools 'promote continuity in learning' between the Foundation Stage and Year 1 by introducing a range of 'key features of good early years practice' into Year 1. But the messages from *Continuing the Learning Journey* were frequently overshadowed by the two national strategies with their conflicting messages about pedagogy and practice. While none of these documents were (or are) statutory, Ofsted paid more attention to the delivery of the national strategies than they did to *Continuing the Learning Journey*, with the result that the more teacher-directed approaches of the strategies gained a stronger foothold than those from the NAA that were promoting more child-initiated learning.

Two more recent national reviews have highlighted further proposals to improve transition to Key Stage 1. *The Independent Review of the Primary Curriculum: Final Report* (DCSF 2009), commissioned by the Secretary of State for Children, Schools and Families and led by Sir Jim Rose, has proposed a number of significant changes to the primary curriculum which will impact on transition at this stage. These include a move away from primary 'subjects' and towards new 'areas of learning' that are intended to be coterminous with those of the new EYFS* (see Figure 1.1).

In addition, Rose makes the following recommendation regarding transition and progression to Key Stage 1:

> *Recommendation 15:* The QCA should make sure that guidance on the revised primary National Curriculum includes clear advice about how best to support those children who need to continue to work towards the early learning goals and build on the learning that has taken place in the EYFS.
>
> (DCSF 2009: 23)

This recommendation is particularly welcome in that the 'Rose Report' is the first official document to acknowledge that most children are not achieving all their Early Learning Goals by the end of the Foundation

---

*It should be noted at this juncture that in September 2008 the 'Foundation Stage' became the EYFS – a single 'quality framework' for children from birth to age 5, whereas the original 'Foundation Stage' was for children age 3 to age 5. There is more information about the EYFS in Chapter 2.

> **Figure 1.1 The areas of learning proposed by *The Independent Review of the Primary Curriculum* (DCSF 2009)**
>
> | 0–5 years (The EYFS) | 5–11 years (The Primary Curriculum) |
> | --- | --- |
> | Communication, language and literacy | English, communication and languages |
> | Personal, social and emotional development | Understanding physical development, health and well-being |
> | Physical development | |
> | Knowledge and understanding of the world | Historical, geographical and social understanding |
> | | Scientific and technological understanding |
> | Creative development | Understanding the arts |
> | Problem-solving, reasoning and numeracy | Understanding mathematics |
> | | ICT across all areas of learning |

Stage, as was the expectation. We will return to this issue and its impact on the Year 1 curriculum in a while.

The second review to address transition is the Cambridge Primary Review led by Professor Robin Alexander. The review team has recently published a report entitled *Towards a New Primary Curriculum: A Report from the Cambridge Primary Review. Part 2: The Future* (available online at www.primaryreview.org.uk/Publications/CambridgePrimaryReviewrep. html). This report identifies the 'top-down' pressure of not just the Primary Curriculum but also the Secondary Curriculum on the early years of education and acknowledges that this is especially the case in relation to literacy:

> Whatever they have separately achieved, the expansion of pre-school provision and the KS1/2 standards agenda has made this vital point of transition increasingly fraught, for it has been squeezed by two very different views of what primary education should be about.
>
> (Alexander 2009: 23)

The Cambridge Review also proposes a new model for the Primary Curriculum based this time on 'domains' which will build on the EYFS areas of learning and lead on to the Key Stage 3 curriculum in secondary education. This review is equally concerned with *how* children learn as much as *what* they should learn and questions policy in England that appears to be premised on the 'questionable principle' that the younger children start formal schooling the better they will eventually do. While pointing out that the experience of those countries whose children start formal schooling up to two years later than in England manage to outperform their English peers by age 11, the review also asserts the following: 'In a world where pre-school education and care are increasingly the norm the argument is less about starting ages than the nature and appropriateness of provision on either side of the line, wherever it is drawn' (Alexander 2009: 5).

This book is entirely concerned with provision and practice that is appropriate to children who are 5 and 6 years of age, and so we move on to what national assessment data is telling us about children's achievements at this age.

National assessment data at the point of transition from Foundation Stage to Key Stage 1

Although the findings of official reports undoubtedly began to affect the way in which LAs and school leadership teams viewed the experiences of children in Year 1, there was one factor that had, perhaps, an even greater influence on attitudes towards current practice.

Since 2004, the government has produced national data based on the outcomes from the administration of the Foundation Stage Profile – the assessment of all children at the end of the Foundation Stage. This data has revealed, year on year, that while the Early Learning Goals are expectations for 'most children' to achieve by the end of the Foundation Stage (a phrase introduced in the original *Curriculum Guidance for the Foundation Stage* and now perpetuated in *The Early Years Foundation Stage* – DCSF 2008), this is far from reality. The data have consistently shown that significant numbers of children move into Year 1 without having achieved all their Early Learning Goals. While none of the Goals are achieved by more than around 50 per cent of children, some Goals have proved particularly hard to achieve and in 2008, for example, the Goal for 'Writing' was achieved by only 24 per cent of all children and the Goals for 'Creative Development' and 'Calculating' were achieved by only 27 per cent. Figures vary about the percentage of children achieving all their Early Learning Goals, but in some LAs (which are nonetheless achieving 'national expectations') the figure is reported to be around 10 per cent, which means that some 90 per cent of children are entering Year 1 classes still needing to complete their Foundation Stage education in certain areas of learning.

Put another way, this means that the vast majority of children across the country are entering Year 1 not developmentally ready to begin the National Curriculum. This has caused a radical rethink in many local authorities and in many schools, and the official institutional view of transition has become a key element of strategic plans for improvement.

Local concerns

Concerns about the experiences of children transferring from the Foundation Stage to Key Stage 1 have not only been expressed through government documentation and statistics. Across the country, many LAs have been conducting their own evaluations of children's experiences as they make this transition, and documenting them in order to improve practice.

Most LAs that have undertaken such an exercise have been concerned to find out the views of their teachers, their children and their parents. One example of this is in Oxfordshire, where the LA supported a three-year research project about the transition of children from Foundation Stage to Year 1 (OCC 2006, 2009).

When Oxfordshire consulted its teachers it found many who were concerned about the appropriateness of children's Year 1 experiences and how significantly they differed from those in the Foundation Stage. Teachers' responses included many comments which were similar to the following.

'It just doesn't feel right. I can see the children are bored and need to be up and playing but we still have to do the Literacy Hour.'

'I can't stand this any more. I just have to find a way of delivering the curriculum in ways that will engage the children.'

'I just know in my bones that what children are getting isn't right for their stage of development. I want to make it more child-friendly.'

The voices of the teachers raised so many concerns that Oxfordshire then consulted its parents. Parents of both Reception and Year 1 children were asked how their children (and they) felt about the move into Year 1. As might be imagined, the parents' responses were more disparate than the teachers'. There were a significant number of parents who were pleased that there would be a difference between Reception and Year 1, particularly among those whose children were yet to transfer.

'I think S. is getting bored with playing now. She's ready to do harder work and to do more reading and writing so I'm pleased she is going into Mrs XX's class.'

'I think we'll both be pleased with the more school activities in year 1. S. wants to learn more reading and writing and can do this better in Year 1.'

'I really think the children have too much freedom in Foundation. I know they learn when they play but I'm not convinced that's what school is for.'

But such responses were not the majority view. Many parents were already expressing anxiety about their child's transition.

'I can see how anxious Josh is getting. He loves outdoors in Foundation and there isn't any outdoors in Year 1.'

'I wish the Year 1 class could be more like Reception. I know they have to learn harder things but need it be so boring?'

'My child doesn't want to go to Year 1. He knows that it's the end of play and he's not ready to sit and listen all the time.'

Interestingly, these concerns were voiced most consistently by parents of children who had already made the transition into Year 1. Here, the messages were more in line with those of the teachers.

'My son was in Year 1 last year and he just got so bored with sitting on the carpet all the time. He needs to be more active if he is going to stay interested in school.'

'All he seems to do is literacy and numeracy. I remember doing projects and topics when I was his age and he doesn't do those at all.'

'I think there should be more time to play in Year 1. They're learning at the same time and it is a better way to learn than sitting and listening to the teacher all the time.'

Finally, in Oxfordshire, the LA consulted the children. Every child in the Reception year in all of the county's schools was sent a questionnaire which asked broadly the same question as the one posed to their teachers and parents. It asked: 'Show us how you feel about moving into Year 1' (see Figure 1.2).

There was space for a drawing and, at the bottom of the paper, some lines above which was written: 'While drawing, the child talked about this . . .', to give the teacher the opportunity to record any significant responses that the drawings might not have portrayed.

In total, 2381 questionnaires were returned. The majority of children wrote about 'looking forward to' Year 1. They drew pictures of what they were looking forward to and wrote about why they were feeling positive. The most frequently cited reasons for this were:

- 'being older' – 'I felt tall because we were going into Year 1 and very happy';
- being able to go onto the big playground – 'I can play football in the big playground and Roger will play';
- doing harder work – 'I would like to learn more difficult spellings'.

Figure 1.2 Questionnaire sent to all Reception class children

show us how you feel...

PLEASE DRAW A PICTURE BELOW ABOUT MOVING INTO YEAR ONE

Whilst drawing, the child talked about this...

OXFORDSHIRE
COUNTY COUNCIL
CHILDREN, YOUNG PEOPLE & FAMILIES
www.oxfordshire.gov.uk

The playground featured significantly in the responses, for as many children spoke about this with trepidation as they did with anticipation.

However, a significant number of children qualified their 'looking forward to' comments with concerns, while some wrote only negatively about their feelings. Nearly a quarter of the responses were either partially or entirely negative, with children talking about 'being sad', 'worried', 'scared', 'nervous' and 'shy'. Other words such as 'frightened', 'angry' and 'cross' were used, but less frequently.

The negative words used by the children seem to fall into two categories: those about feelings of 'leaving behind' what was loved and familiar, and those about feelings of 'anxiety' about what was to come. Being sad about leaving things behind is entirely natural and shows that staff in the Foundation Stage had established the warm and reciprocal relationships that typify good early years environments. So there was regret about leaving:

- teachers and teaching assistants – 'I'm sad because I love Miss XXX and I don't want go';
- friends who may be going to another class – 'I'm sad because Gemma is going to another class and I can't go with her';
- toys, equipment and environments – 'I'm sad because I'm going to miss the teepee and the sandpit'.

However, the remaining half of the negative responses expressed fears about what was to come and gave the class teachers greater cause for concern.

'I'm worried about the big playground, the big children might push me over.'

'I feel nervous about my new teacher and I don't know her.'

'I'm scared because I am going to a room I don't know.'

'I have to sit on the bigger people's table at lunchtime.'

The children's responses spurred on the class teachers to think more seriously about transition from the children's perspective. Many of the Project teachers realised that they had *assumed* how children would be feeling – and that, in some cases, their assumptions had been wrong. There were children whom they had thought would be looking forward to the move who were expressing anxieties and, conversely, children whom they thought would be apprehensive about transition who were anticipating it with eagerness.

The questionnaires led teachers in the Project to come up with a variety of ideas about how to improve transition for their children, and the results of their thinking can be read about in Chapter 3. In addition, the questionnaires had such an impact on their practice that many of the teachers decided that they would consult every future class in the same way, because they understood that each class is made up of differing individuals with different feelings about transition.

Child development

All of the concerns raised above have been based on evidence gleaned from observation of some kind. In some cases, the observations were carried out by official figures such as Ofsted inspectors or researchers. In some cases, the observations were undertaken by teachers or parents. In other cases, the observations would contribute to the completion of the Foundation Stage Profile. But it is important to remember that there are other assessments that have been made of children over time that have impacted on our understanding of how children develop and have contributed to the profession's knowledge about how *all* children develop and how *all* children learn.

Effective practice is usually effective because it harnesses approaches that are developmentally appropriate for children. This means that planning will start from the current needs, interests and capacities of children, rather than from a certain page in a file that suggests that all children receive the same 'diet' because they happen to be in the same class. It means that planning is rooted in ongoing, systematic observation of each child as a learner rather than being rooted in a sequence of units of work that move on relentlessly regardless of children's learning needs or their levels of understanding. It is concerned with the developmental *stage* each child has reached, rather than making assumptions according to a child's *age*.

A core principle of the EYFS is that children are 'unique'. It acknowledges that 'children develop and learn in different ways and at different rates' (DCSF 2008: para. 1.11) and practitioners are expected to take this fully into account when they plan for children's individual learning experiences. How can this be the case when children are in the Reception year and not when they are in Year 1? How can it be that a Reception child is entitled to 'be supported individually to make progress at their own pace' (DCSF 2008: para. 1.13) when Year 1 children are often required to meet universal outcomes to whole-class objectives?

If we are looking to strengthen our rationale for reviewing current practice in Year 1, then it is crucial to remember (or reconsider) the following facts from the child development literature.

- *A class of children is not a homogeneous group of learners.* Every teacher knows that within their class there is a vast range of children with a vast range of learning needs and abilities. It is simply not sensible to suggest that teachers plan for a whole class as though all the children need the same thing at the same time. Chapter 4 will look in greater depth at the issue of whole-class teaching and its relevance for Key Stage 1 children but, for now, suffice to say that children are just as 'unique' in Year 1 as they are in Reception, and should be treated as such.

- *The learning of young children is neither linear nor predictable.* Young children's learning journeys are individual and idiosyncratic. Sometimes children have a spurt of development; sometimes they come to a grinding halt and remain on a plateau; sometimes they go back and revisit something in order to sort out a misunderstanding. They do not do this in synchrony. When one child is shooting forwards, another may be consolidating and revisiting; when one child understands something, another may need several additional experiences and opportunities to come to a similar level of understanding; while some children have previous experiences or knowledge to draw on, for others a concept or skill can be completely new. Every child is a complex fusion of experience (from home far more than school), aptitudes, attitudes and interests. How can we suggest that all children in one class who were taught 'X' today, will all need 'Y' tomorrow?

- *Developmentally, there is very little difference between a Reception child and a Year 1 child.* All of the child development literature that concerns children of this age says that the key changes in children's development come around the end of Year 2 when children approach the age of 7. Nowhere in the literature does it say that suddenly, at age 6 children prefer to learn by listening to the teacher. Nowhere does it say that children learn best when they are sitting on a carpet. Nowhere does it say that children no longer need play and no longer like learning out of doors. In fact, the literature is unequivocal in saying that children's learning needs at age 6 are pretty much the same as at age 5, so as teachers we need to be asking whether current practices and opportunities in Year 1 classrooms reflect the active and interactive children we see learning in the Foundation Stage. Chapter 2 explores how children learn at this age in greater depth. It also introduces Year 1 teachers to the basic principles of the EYFS on which their practice should build.

Conclusions

The difference between current practice in Reception and Year 1 classes has largely been brought about by successive initiatives that have not taken the developmental needs of children into account. In particular, children in Year 1 have been subjected to initiatives that have been introduced for the whole 'primary' age span without sufficient consideration being given to whether these initiatives are appropriate for 5-year-old learners. Child development tells us that children's learning needs in Year 1 are broadly similar to those for children in the Reception year and that children should not go from being seen as a 'unique child' (DCSF 2008) to a 'Year 1' in one small step down the school corridor.

Things to discuss in your school

- What are the similarities and differences between children's experiences in Reception and Year 1?

- Are these differences based on what you believe about children's learning?

- What evidence is there, from Foundation Stage Profile outcomes, of the range of learning needs of children moving into your Year 1 class(es)?

2

How do 5–7-year-olds learn?

Introduction

If you search through child development books about the ways in which 5- and 6-year-old children learn you do not find very much! At least you find very little that discriminates in any way between learners of 5 or 6 years of age.

A considerable amount has been written about the development of babies and toddlers as they make gargantuan strides in their understanding of the world and their place within it. A significant amount has also been written about children around the age of 7-plus as they move from more concrete to more abstract ways of learning, something we will come to later on. But, in between, there is very little to discriminate the 5-year-old learner from the 6-year-old learner. Largely, of course, because – in terms of human development – nothing very spectacular happens between those two birthdays.

So, let's begin by seeing what the child development literature *does* say about children between the ages of 5 and 7.

Stages of development

Many psychologists have attempted to describe young children's learning in developmental stages, suggesting that between 'this' age and 'that' age, certain key understandings, skills or behaviours become apparent. Probably the best known and, in education circles, the most referred to theory of 'stage' development belongs to the Swiss biologist and psychologist Jean Piaget (1896–1980). Piaget's theory concerned the role of maturation in children's increasing capacity to understand their world.

Our 5- and 6-year-olds come in the middle of what Piaget (1952) termed the 'preoperational stage' – from age 2 to 7 years – when, he suggests, the child learns to use language and to represent objects by images and words; when their thinking is still egocentric and they have difficulty taking the viewpoint of others; when they continue to classify objects by a single feature (e.g. grouping together all the circles regardless of colour).

Many psychologists replicated Piaget's experiments and subsequently found flaws in the way in which children were presented with tasks (see particularly Donaldson 1978) and, therefore, criticized Piaget's 'stages' for misrepresenting children's abilities. However, it is still worthy of note that it was at age 7 that Piaget believed children move to a more 'concrete operational' stage of development – when they become able to think more logically about objects and events and think in more abstract ways (see Figure 2.1 for more detail).

More recent literature on child development treats 5-, 6- and 7-year-old learners as 'one phase'. Bredekamp (1987), for example, describes children and their developmental characteristics from age 5 to 8 years; Lindon (1993) from age 5 to 7 years; Tassoni (2007) from 6 to 9 years; and Robinson (2008) from 5 to 8 years. These authors see so many overlaps in the characteristics of children within these age groups that they do not attempt to discriminate more finely between one year group and another.

While there are no significant differences between a 5- and a 6-year-old learner, there *are* often differences *between* learners who are 5 years of age, or indeed 6 years of age. Our own experience, as well as the literature, tells us that children within one year group are, in developmental terms, very different. Just because they are 'in Year 1' does not mean that they have the same abilities or learning needs as other children in the same class. So it is understandable that psychologists and writers do not attempt to describe developmental characteristics as though they were discrete to one particular year group.

However, within these broader age phases, the spurt in development around age 7 is frequently pointed out. Drawing on the literature above, for example, we see the particular developmental surge that happens around the end of Year 2.

There is, in fact, one series of books – from the Tavistock Clinic in London – that attempts to describe children's characteristics per year of birth (e.g. Holdich 1992; Steiner 1993; Osborne 1997). As you would expect, however, the characteristics ascribed to a typical 5-year-old – for example, acquiring independence; asking questions of the environment;

Figure 2.1 How children's learning develops *around* age 7

- Children think more logically (Bredekamp 1987).
- Children think in more abstract ways (they do not always have to touch or move objects in order to understand them) (Bredekamp 1987).
- Children solve problems in their heads (Piaget 1952; Piaget and Inhelder 1969).
- Children are increasingly drawn to adults initiating learning (rather than always wanting to investigate their own ideas and interests) (Bredekamp 1987); girls may be ready before boys (Robinson 2008).
- Children become more literate (Robinson 2008):

  o by age 7 they are able to track across a whole page;
  o from about age 6 they read increasingly with understanding of vocabulary and 'proper' sentences (some will do this earlier and some take much longer);
  o by around age 6 their wrist bones are usually fully developed allowing finer control over writing tasks (Tassoni 2007);
  o by around age 7 a 'mature' grasp for holding pencils etc. is established.

- Children develop their metacognitive skills (using their 'thinking about thinking' to improve their learning) (Tassoni 2007).
- Children understand opposites such as short-long, sharp-blunt (Robinson 2008).
- Children are able to take another's point of view (which enhances their skills of communication) but still tend to see things in terms of 'black' and 'white' (Bredekamp 1987; Robinson 2008).
- Children seek approval of peers as well as adults (can have strong friendships and sometimes 'enemies') (Robinson 2008).
- Children are generally cooperative and games with rules become increasingly popular (Robinson 2008).
- Children like projects, collecting and more complicated games (Robinson 2008).

taking steps to interact with others; concern for rules; developing motor skills; still at a concrete stage of thinking – could be applied to many 6-year-olds also – and indeed to many 4-year-olds as well. So it is understandable that psychologists and writers alike do not attempt to pin down developmental characteristics too tightly between the ages of 5 and 7, and acknowledge that the age of a child does not assign him a homogenous set of abilities and attributes common to all other children of the same age.

However, the developmental surge at age 7 is well worth noting. Firstly, we should remind ourselves that, from the beginning of Key Stage 2, children can manage new, more abstract ways of learning – although this does not mean, of course, that they no longer need concrete, first-hand, hands-on experiences at times as well. Secondly, the common reference to a developmental surge at age 7 reminds us also of the *absence* of any evidence of a developmental surge between the ages of 5 and 7. This means that there is no rationale for the approaches to learning and teaching that are seen to be appropriate for a child in the Reception class being *in*appropriate for a child in Year 1 or Year 2.

We need to truly 'continue the learning journey' from the Foundation Stage to Year 1. This does not mean that children's learning will stand still or that standards will decline. But what the child development literature informs us is that *how* children learn should not be very different in a Key Stage 1 class than it is in a Reception class; that what is deemed to be 'developmentally appropriate' practice in the Foundation Stage remains every bit as developmentally appropriate in Key Stage 1.

Developmentally appropriate practice

In Chapter 1 we learned that there is an irrefutable logic in basing strategies for learning and teaching on what is most suited to a child's stage of development. If children are ready to learn something (not necessarily on their own, but sometimes with skilful adult help), and if they learn it in ways that suit their preferred ways of learning, then that learning is more likely to be successful. When children are more motivated to learn, this has a profound impact on learning outcomes (Bandura 1977; Dweck 1978). If, on the other hand, children are put into learning situations which do not match their preferred ways of learning and do not allow them to be the kind of learners they naturally are, then the chances are that learning will not be as effective. So, what do we need to know about a child's stage of development in order to decide what will be developmentally appropriate provision?

The concept of developmental appropriateness has two dimensions. The excellent text edited by Bredekamp back in 1987 helpfully separates out what is 'age appropriate' from what is 'individually appropriate'. Bredekamp writes the following.

1 **Age appropriateness.** Human development research indicates that there are universal, predictable sequences of growth and change that occur in children during the first 9 years of life. These predictable changes occur in all domains of development – physical, emotional, social, and cognitive. Knowledge of typical development of children within the age span . . . provides a framework from which teachers prepare and plan appropriate experiences.

2 **Individual appropriateness.** Each child is a unique person with an individual pattern and timing of growth, as well as individual personality, learning style, and family background. Both the curriculum and adults' interactions with children should be responsive to individual differences. Learning in young children is the result of interaction between the child's thoughts and experiences with materials, ideas, and people. These experiences should match the child's developing abilities, while also challenging the child's interest and understanding.

(Bredekamp 1987 p.2)

So, although universal and predictable sequences of human development appear to exist, a major premise of developmentally appropriate practice is that each child is unique and so developmentally appropriate practice needs to recognize the enormous variance that exists in the timing of individual development that is within the normal range.

Year 1 teachers involved in the second phase of the Oxfordshire Transition Project (OCC 2009) agreed their own definition of developmentally appropriate practice (see Figure 2.2). This definition turned into a set of guiding principles underpinning the development of Year 1 practice that built seamlessly on children's previous experience.

A definition such as this can be seen instantly to establish a very different pedagogy from that currently operating in many Year 1 classes. In the Oxfordshire Project we began by asking what is currently the same

---

Figure 2.2 Oxfordshire Transition Project's definition of developmentally appropriate practice

'Practice that starts from the current needs, interests and capacities of children and is rooted in on-going, systematic observation of each child as a learner. It is concerned with the developmental stage each child has reached rather than making assumptions according to a child's age.'

---

and what is different about Reception and Year 1 practice. The answers of the Project teachers – and indeed of thousands of other teachers to whom we have posed this question – suggest that developmentally appropriate practice (as defined in Figure 2.1) is not currently the norm in the majority of Key Stage 1 classrooms.

The list below (Figure 2.3) is a composite from the answers given to the question – 'What is currently the same and what different in Reception and Year 1 practice in your school'? It may be that these answers are not typical of your school – but, on the other hand, you may well recognize the differences that these teachers have identified. The issues included in the list are those that have come up again and again when this question is posed at inservice training sessions.

It is important to say at this juncture that not all Foundation Stage or Reception teachers will 'recognize' the column on the left. In some schools it would not necessarily be appropriate to aim to 'build on' the Foundation Stage because the Foundation Stage practice is not yet good enough. So, it would be just as interesting for your Reception teacher to see whether their practice includes those aspects of best practice identified by other Foundation Stage teachers. Either way, the lists should be a good catalyst for a discussion between Foundation Stage and Year 1 staff.

The list in Figure 2.3 shows up the many differences and discrepancies between children's learning experiences in the Foundation Stage and in Year 1. It is quite clear that when the national initiatives that led to these different ways of learning were designed, no one thought through what it would be like for a child to make the transition from the one key stage to the next. As we have seen earlier in this chapter, there is no good developmental reason why children's experiences should be any different in Reception and Year 1 – and yet teachers up and down the country report differences such as these that have a profound impact on how children learn and, therefore, how effectively they learn.

Figure 2.3 Differences between practice in many Reception and Year 1 classes, identified by a range of teachers

Reception	Year 1
Have an outdoor area for learning	Usually do not have an outdoor area
Have considerable indoor space for active learning	Often have smaller classrooms with a table and chair for each child
Have a wide range of resources for play-based learning	Have a lot of subject-based resources but few for play
Have ratios of at least 1 adult to 15 children	The teacher is often the only adult
Have free-flow learning without breaks in the morning or afternoon session	Follow a compartmentalized timetable where children frequently change what they are doing (e.g. literacy followed by playtime followed by numeracy followed by assembly etc.)
Learning experiences offer a balance between adult-initiated and child-initiated activity	Learning is adult-directed
Play is the key way in which children learn	'Play' is often offered to children to fill in moments before break or assembly or when the teacher's work is finished
Learning is active, practical, hands-on and first-hand	Learning is often abstract – either 'through' the teacher or through worksheets
Children work most often in small groups, in pairs or alone, on a range of cross-curriculum activities	Children work frequently as a whole class, either together on the carpet or carrying out small group tasks from a common whole-class learning objective

Children move fluidly between groups according to preference and differentiation relevant to the current activity	Children are in often in fixed groups for all learning – particularly literacy and numeracy
Children are highly independent in their learning and in using the learning environment	Children become more dependent on the teacher to tell them what to do
Parents contribute to their child's assessment profiles	Parents are usually informed about their child's progress on formal occasions such as parents' evenings
The Foundation Stage is recognized as 'a distinct phase' and there is growing understanding (from other staff) of an 'appropriate' early years curriculum	Teachers are often pressurized to 'get children ready for SATs' (especially by Year 2 teachers)
Planning addresses all areas of learning equally across the curriculum	Have to produce separate more detailed plans for literacy and numeracy
Planning is based on children's interests	Planning is based on schemes of work and guidance from national strategies
Evidence of learning is based on observation of children, conversations with them and their parents, photographs and so on	Evidence is frequently gathered from children's books (collected in order to 'track progress' through a subject)
Parents understand why children are playing to learn	Parents often expect to see more formal ways of learning and more work in books
Reception children are allowed to have different organizational arrangements (e.g. for assembly, playtime, uniform)	Year 1 are expected to be 'part of the school'

How Key Stage 1 teachers believe their children learn best

If so many Year 1 teachers are uncomfortable about how their children are currently learning, what are the ways in which they believe their children would learn more effectively? Earlier in the chapter we drew together some evidence from the child development literature about how children learn naturally when they are 5, 6 and 7 years of age. But, whatever the literature suggests, only teachers can make that final decision about how they believe their children learn and, therefore, what strategies to employ in their own classrooms. Only individual teachers know their children well enough to say, 'This is how I am going to plan and organize the learning in my classroom.'

In many ways this is an important point to emphasize. Many teachers say they feel torn between one set of expectations and the next. Torn, for example, between their headteacher and the parents. Between the early years advisory teams and the literacy and numeracy advisory teams. Torn between the School Improvement Partner (SIP) and Ofsted. Education at the current time can feel a very confusing and conflicting place to be. But, at the end of the day, I have always believed that when you are being pulled between a pillar and a post there is only once place to look – at the children. Initiatives may come and go, policies may change – but the children and how they learn remain constant (it is only our *understanding* of how they learn that changes and, hopefully, deepens over time).

The same teachers who helped to compile the list of differences in practice (Figure 2.3) also had very strong views about how their children learned best (see Figure 2.4). These teachers were not drawing on child development literature, but on the first-hand evidence of being alongside their own children day in, day out – the most compelling kind of evidence a teacher can use.

Before looking at Figure 2.4, you may want to write down your own views and then compare these with what other teachers have written below.

Figure 2.4 How Year 1 and 2 teachers believe their children learn best

Naturally and spontaneously

⮕ When playing

⮕ Using all their senses

⮕ Being outside

⮕ Informally (as well as formally)

⮕ Through real-life experiences

⮕ Finding things out for themselves

⮕ Investigating

⮕ Grappling

⮕ Being inquisitive

⮕ Being messy and creative

⮕ Through open-ended investigation

Seeing the world in different ways

Given time and space
- Having sufficient space for active learning
- Outdoor space as well as indoor
- Access to outdoor space all day
- Flexible space that can be used for a variety of activities
- Time to see an activity through
- Time to go wrong and put it right again
- Time to 'get into' an activity and not be rushed
- Time to finish rather than be stopped halfway through

When motivated by
- Being excited
- New experiences
- Bringing stuff from home
- Learning being fun
- Learning pitched at the right level
- Having choice and variety
- Taking risks and succeeding!
- A rich environment
- Not being too tired
- Being encouraged to be independent
- Having choices
- Valuing their own achievements (rather than getting the teacher's 'gold star')
- Using different styles of learning to suit different occasions

Supported by knowledgeable adults
- By being shown (by adults as well as children)
- By the teacher making connections
- When adults respond to them rather than direct learning
- When adults scaffold their learning
- When they are responded to positively
- Through short adult 'blasts'
- Experiencing a balance between play and adult-led learning

⟫ When adults have time to teach rather than being rushed

⟫ When adults listen to and respect their contributions

⟫ When adults build on previous experiences

⟫ When adults intervene appropriately

Alongside peers

⟫ From each other

⟫ By being shown (by adults as well as children)

⟫ Talking together

⟫ Negotiating and testing out together

⟫ Through genuine collaboration that requires 'teamwork'

⟫ By watching and seeing 'what's possible'

⟫ By having more confidence to put ideas forward

⟫ Because children prefer listening to another child than an adult

⟫ Because learning alongside peers requires different skills than learning alongside adults

Having time to talk to others

By initiating their own enquiries

⮕ By asking questions

⮕ By making their own connections

⮕ By pursuing their own interests

⮕ By representing their own ideas and strategies

⮕ By drawing on their own experiences

⮕ Having a purpose (theirs!)

⮕ When the learning is important to *them*

⮕ When *they* ask for the knowledge *they* need

⮕ Through ownership of the curriculum and activities

⮕ Through making their own judgements about how well they have achieved something

Rehearsing and repeating

⮕ Practising what is new

⮕ Practising what is familiar

⮕ Revisiting concepts and skills rather than just moving on

⮕ Having time to come back to something and learn it in a different way

⮕ Meeting experiences in different ways rather than always the same way

⮕ Gaining self-confidence from rehearsing what has been done before

⮕ Using familiar skills in unfamiliar situations

⮕ Consolidating and 'composting' (Claxton 1997)

⮕ Trying again when things are hard

⮕ Persevering and having time to keep 'at it'

In a relaxed, supportive atmosphere

⮕ Being happy

⮕ Being relaxed

- Being loved and cared for
- When enjoying themselves
- When not having to get answers 'right' in front of the whole class
- Through making mistakes (without fear of being told off or told they are 'wrong')
- Through being confident in putting forward their own ideas
- By being given time to think
- When they are comfortable
- When they are prepared to take risks
- When they are in the right state of mind
- When they are feeling safe
- When they are heard and respected
- When they are listened to
- When their self-esteem is high
- When they are settled
- When relationships are good
- When home life isn't worrying them
- When secure in their routines

When engaged and involved

- When things relate to their own experiences
- When learning is relevant and meaningful
- When they are challenged
- Being inspired
- Being stimulated
- When learning is not predictable or too routine
- By having some say in what is done or how it is done
- By being encouraged to use their own initiative

As so often happens, teachers' own theories about what works best in their classrooms are based on the evidence of their own eyes. Yet, while this may be so, this first-hand evidence chimes so closely with what robust research evidence also says. There are good reasons why what teachers believe to be the most effective ways in which their children learn is borne out in the child development literature – and vice versa. Best practice is informed by the constant cycle of observation, action and reflection and is based on what children naturally and spontaneously do best to achieve what they want. The most effective teachers draw on this to inform their approaches to learning and teaching across the curriculum.

What is clear to see is that neither in the literature nor amongst teachers' own beliefs about learning is there anything that suggests that children learn most effectively when:

- they are sitting endlessly on the carpet;
- when they are learning predominantly as part of a whole-class group;
- when they are listening to an adult's ideas rather than offering their own;
- when they are engaged exclusively in adult-initiated activities.

Yet this is exactly how Year 1 teachers described the key elements of their practice when the Oxfordshire Transition Project began. While practice in Key Stage 1 is no longer as compartmentalized and homogenized as it was a few years ago, nevertheless Figure 2.2 reminds us that Year 1 teachers still face considerable constraints and barriers to achieving the kind of developmentally appropriate practice they believe suits their children.

Learning age 5–7 in other countries of the UK

It is interesting to note that in other countries of the UK there has been a recognition that education at age 5 to 7 should not be separated out from education at age 3 to 5.

Wales

In 2008, the Welsh Assembly introduced a 'Foundation Phase' of education for children from age 3 to the end of Key Stage 1 (age 7). The *Framework for Children's Learning* (DCELLS 2008) makes the principled statement that 'a curriculum for young children should be appropriate to their stage of learning rather than focusing solely on age-related outcomes to be achieved' (p. 4).

The monitoring and evaluation of the implementation of the Foundation Phase Project (Siraj-Blatchford *et al.* 2006) re-emphasizes these points when it states:

> A major assumption that has informed the amalgamation of the current Early Years and KS1 into the new Foundation Phase in Wales, where it is intended that children's development and learning will be seen as a continuum from 3–7, has been that there is no real reason for considering the development of children in two stages – under fives and over fives. Lindon (1993) has argued this later stage is merely a continuum of the first stage of child development. This belief is also supported by effective practice in a number of international contexts, where children begin formal education at a later age than in the UK.
>
> (Siraj-Blatchford *et al.* 2006: 102)

Scotland

In Scotland, too, there have been moves towards the preschool sector and the early years of primary schooling being 'presented together as one level'. The principles and rationale for this new approach are set out in the document *Curriculum for Excellence* and the emphasis is on active learning which is defined as 'Children . . . doing, thinking and exploring, and (learning) through quality interaction, intervention and relationships' (Scottish Executive 2008):

> Research indicates that developmentally appropriate practice is most conducive to effective learning. For example, it suggests that there is no long-term advantage to children when there is an over-emphasis on systematic teaching before 6 or 7 years of age. A key message is that approaches to fostering learning need to be flexible to take account of the needs of the child, and will change as children develop.
>
> (Scottish Executive 2008: 2)

Northern Ireland

In Northern Ireland *The Revised Curriculum* (Council for the Curriculum, Examinations and Assessment 2007) was rolled out during 2006–7 in the following stages: Foundation Stage, Years 1 and 2 (children aged 4 years 2 months to 6 years); Key Stage 2, Years 3 and 4; and Key Stage 3, years 5, 6 and 7. Preschool education or early years provision in Northern Ireland is presently separate, with its own curriculum because it is non-statutory provision. However, the Foundation Stage ethos and practice is modelled on existing preschool practice and is seen to be creating more cohesion between the sectors. Northern Ireland is presently undergoing a 0–6 strategy review in which it is believed many issues will be considered in order to provide a more unified service. The review was undertaken following the transfer of responsibilities in November 2006, when the Department of Education became entirely responsible for preschool provision for the first time.

The Revised Curriculum emphasizes the following:

> Children learn best when learning is interactive, practical and enjoyable . . . In the Foundation Stage children should experience much of their learning through well-planned and challenging play. Self-initiated play helps children to understand and learn about themselves and their surroundings. Motivation can be increased when children have opportunities to make choices and decisions about their learning, particularly when their own ideas and interests are used, either as starting points for learning activities or for pursuing a topic in more depth.
>
> (Council for the Curriculum, Examinations and Assessment, 2007: 1.7, 9)

Learning age 5–7 in other countries of the world

England is not only out of step with other countries in the UK. In comparison to many other countries around the world, the school starting age in England is low. Parents are required to ensure their children receive full-time education from the term after their fifth birthday. The age of 5 was first introduced into English legislation as part of the 1870 Education Act (Woodhead 1989) when decisions were made that were more concerned about issues of child protection and the age at which children should enter the workforce, rather than the age at which it might be best for them to start formal education. In practice, of course, increasing numbers of children in England are now being admitted to primary school well before their fifth birthday. Most LAs have moved from a three-term entry throughout the Reception year to a single point of entry in the September of the year in which the child becomes 5 – a policy currently being promoted by Sir Jim Rose in his *Independent Review of the Primary Curriculum* (DCSF 2009).

Yet in most countries in Europe, children do not begin compulsory schooling until the age of 6 or 7. Statistics provided by the European Commission (reported in Sharp 2002) show that over half of the 33 European countries investigated have age 6 as the official school starting age and in three Scandinavian countries and five eastern European countries the starting age is 7.

But does an earlier start to school mean an improvement in children's academic achievement? Do English children in Key Stage 1 do better in national comparisons because they have already had two to three additional years of statutory schooling? The evidence base is complex but, from her extensive research, Sharp (2002: 15) concludes that 'The arguments in favour of children being taught earlier do not appear to be borne out by the evidence'. There *is* evidence that children who have three terms in Reception often do better than those who have had one term (Tymms *et al.* 1997, 2000). But this is generally because those three-term children are older, not because they are more able. More important to note perhaps is that younger children – those born in the summer term – do not do as well as their autumn-born peers even when they have three terms in Reception (Sharp and Hutchinson 1997).

As Sharp (1998) points out, international comparisons are indirect evidence at best, because they involve such different cultures and education systems. Such complex, multi-layered research can be used to prove (or disprove) a number of points. However, it is worth reporting that one international study (Elley 1992) that measured reading standards in 32 educational systems found that the top ten scoring countries had a later starting age (the mean starting age being 6.3 years). When the data were analysed, controlling for each country's level of 'economic development' (how well off they were), the trend for older starting ages to be associated with better results was reversed. However, the differences were small and, most significantly, children in the 'later starting' countries had largely caught up by the time they reached the age of 9.

So, there is no firm evidence that starting school earlier benefits children in any significant way and, some research suggests, an early starting age can sometimes be detrimental to children's learning and development.

What matters most of all is not the age at which children start school, but whether their experiences once they are *in* school are appropriate to their age and stage of development. We return to the main theme of this book – that the most effective educational experiences for children are those that are developmentally appropriate for them, where the curriculum is designed to meet the child and not where the child is expected to fit into the curriculum.

Continuing the Learning Journey

In Chapter 1, it was explained that the NAA has produced a document called *Continuing the Learning Journey* (NAA 2005), intended to give Year 1 teachers guidance on how to build effectively on children's Foundation Stage experiences. The document remains a very valuable resource all

Year 1 teachers are encouraged to find their school copy and refer to it. In the meantime, there are several aspects of the document that that will be referred to here, in order to give Year 1 teachers, with little knowledge of good early years practice, some useful information.

The material in *Continuing the Learning Journey* is organized into four sections which encourage Foundation Stage and Year 1 teachers to discuss how children's experiences can become more seamless as they move on into Key Stage 1.

1 Learning from the Foundation Stage

This section identifies features of best practice which the document suggests Year 1 teachers should consider when planning their own provision. All of these issues will be addressed in greater depth in later chapters of this book. Some key features of good early years practice are suggested as being:

- curriculum which is relevant to children;
- first-hand experience;
- learning using senses and movement;
- play;
- learning inside and outside the classroom;
- work at length and depth;
- organization which allows independence;
- partnership with parents and carers;
- observation-led assessment.

2 Continuing the learning

This section draws on DVD material and asks:

- What do these children *see* that is the same in Year 1 and Reception?
- What do these children *experience* that is the same in Year 1 and Reception?
- Who do these children *encounter* both in Year 1 and in Reception?
- In what ways has leadership and management influenced a smooth transition from the Foundation Stage to Key Stage 1 for these children?

3 Learning from children

This section draws on DVD examples of how teachers learn about children and endeavour to plan a relevant curriculum for them based on this knowledge. It asks Year 1 teachers to consider:

- how practitioners build on what is already known about children;
- how practitioners learn about children;
- how practitioners involve children in planning their own learning.

4 The Foundation Stage Profile and school improvement

This final section uses graphs of assessment scales for two different aspects of learning in the Foundation Stage. It aims to show how the outcomes of the Foundation Stage Profile (now the EYFS Profile) can be used to:

- identify strengths and points for improvement in provision in the Foundation Stage;
- inform school improvement planning;
- provide comparisons of achievement for different groups – for example, by gender, ethnicity, English as an additional language;
- make the curriculum in Year 1 responsive to children's needs;
- support performance management.

While the Foundation Stage Profile has now been replaced by the EYFS Profile, the principles which underpin *Continuing the Learning Journey* remain as robust as ever and it will prove a valuable document for any school seriously looking to improve transition from the EYFS into Key Stage 1.

The EYFS

If Key Stage 1 is to build seamlessly on the EYFS, then it is vital that Year 1 teachers are knowledgeable about, and sympathetic to, the curriculum in this initial phase of education. The EYFS (DCSF 2008) was introduced in September 2008 and superseded all other early years documentation then in use. It contains a statutory framework, setting out the standards for learning, development and care for children from birth to 5, as well as a number of guidance documents.

The EYFS must be used by all schools and settings in receipt of the nursery education grant from the government whether they are in the maintained, independent or voluntary sectors. Receipt of this grant also means that the school or setting must agree to be inspected by Ofsted.

The EYFS brings together and replaces three existing early years guidance documents – *Birth to Three Matters, Curriculum Guidance for the Foundation Stage* and the *National Standards for Under 8s Day Care and Childminders.*

The overarching aim of the EYFS is to help young children achieve the five *Every Child Matters* outcomes of:

- staying safe;
- being healthy;
- enjoying and achieving;
- making a positive contribution;
- achieving economic well-being.

The principles underpinning the EYFS have four distinct but complementary themes (DCSF 2008: para. 1.11):

- *A unique child:* recognizes that every child is a competent learner from birth who can be resilient, capable, confident and self-assured.
- *Positive relationships:* describes how children learn to be strong and independent from a base of loving and secure relationships with parents and/or a key person.
- *Enabling environments:* explains that the environment plays a key role in supporting and extending children's development and learning.
- *Learning and development:* recognizes that children develop and learn in different ways and at different rates, and that all areas of learning and development are equally important and interconnected.

The Childcare Act 2006 provides for the EYFS learning and development requirements to comprise three elements (DCSF 2008: para. 2.3):

- *The Early Learning Goals:* the knowledge, skills and understanding which young children should have acquired by the end of the academic year in which they reach the age of 5.
- *The educational programme:* the matters, skills and processes which are required to be taught to young children.
- *The assessment arrangements:* the arrangements for assessing young children to ascertain their achievements.

Figure 2.5 The different aspects of the EYFS six areas of learning and development

Personal, social and emotional development (PSED)

1 Dispositions and attitudes
2 Self-confidence and self-esteem
3 Making relationships
4 Behaviour and self-control
5 Self-care
6 Sense of community

Communication, language and literacy (CLL)

1 Language for communication
2 Language for thinking
3 Linking sounds and letters
4 Reading
5 Writing
6 Handwriting

Problem-solving, reasoning and numeracy (PRN)

1 Numbers as labels and for counting
2 Calculating
3 Shape, space and measures

Knowledge and understanding of the world (KUW)

1 Exploration and investigation
2 Designing and making
3 ICT
4 Time
5 Place
6 Communities

Physical development (PD)

1 Movement and space
2 Health and bodily awareness
3 Using equipment and materials

Creative development (CD)

1 Responding to experiences, expressing and communicating ideas
2 Exploring media and ideas
3 Creating music and dance
4 Developing imagination and imaginative play

There are six areas covered by the Early Learning Goals and education programmes (DCSF 2008: para. 2.4):

- personal, social and emotional development (PSED);
- communication, language and literacy (CLL);

- problem-solving, reasoning and numeracy (PRN);
- knowledge and understanding of the world (KUW);
- physical development (PD);
- creative development (CD).

The six areas are broken down into different aspects as shown in Figure 2.5.

At the end of the EYFS all children are assessed. The EYFS Profile must be completed for each child at the end of their Reception year. The EYFS Profile sums up each child's development and learning and is based on observation and assessment in all six areas of learning and development. Each child's level of development must be recorded against the 13 assessment scales derived from the Early Learning Goals (DCSF 2008: para. 2.21).

Conclusions

So, how do teachers go about continuing children's learning journey from the Foundation Stage to Key Stage 1? If Key Stage 1 is to build seamlessly on the EYFS, then there are two crucial stages in the process of transition for which teachers in both the Foundation Stage and Key Stage 1 need to plan and prepare. Firstly, teachers in both key stages need to consider what they can do to prepare children for the move into Year 1, and this will be addressed in Chapter 3. Then, once children are in Year 1, teachers need to ensure that their practice is developmentally appropriate for the children coming into their classes. This will be addressed in Chapters 4–9.

Things to discuss in your school

- What evidence do you have of the ways in which your children learn best?
- Do you notice any difference in the learning of children in Year 2 as opposed to Year 1?
- Is your practice developmentally appropriate for the children in your class?

CHAPTER 3

Preparing children for the move to Key Stage 1

Introduction

In Chapter 1, we heard the voices of some children expressing their concerns about the move to Key Stage 1. While many of the children were looking forward to 'being older', there were those for whom the impending transition was causing anxiety and apprehension. Of course, transitions of any kind can be met with either uncertainty or eager anticipation. There are those who find moving on to be exciting and stimulating, people who like change, who thrive on new experiences and who have the confidence to meet new challenges. But for others, transitions dredge up old fears and current uncertainties. Such people may not have developed the protective factors that enable them to adapt to new situations, and this can put them at risk of a sequence of negative experiences. It is harder than we think to anticipate how different children will react to change. What teachers need to do is ensure that they know their children sufficiently well to give them all the support they need to make the move to Year 1 as positive as it can be.

Knowing children well

In Chapter 1, we saw one way of getting to know children's feelings about moving into Year 1 (Figure 1.2). Whatever strategy is used, it is important to find out about children's feelings concerning transition and not make assumptions about what they might be. There can be all sorts of reasons why a child may manage better than we anticipate, or struggle when we thought they would be fine.

Children, like adults, can be ready for transitions – or not – at different points in their lives. A child who is usually buoyant and up for a challenge may have just experienced a life event that makes them vulnerable and uncertain. The death of a family member or a pet, separation from a parent through bereavement or the demands of that parent's job, acrimony in the home due to loss of employment, drug or alcohol abuse, can all cause even the most resilient child to find changes at school too much to bear at that particular time.

Regrettably, for some children, transition is not just something to be dealt with at a particular moment, but is a painful and constant factor of their lives. There are children in our classes who are repeatedly taken into care and then returned to their birth families. There are those who are removed, often in the middle of the night, to a refuge and then returned home only to leave once again some days or weeks later. There are children who, because of illness in the family, are sent to the homes of other family members – maybe many miles from their own home – and then returned to their parents, often without being given reasons or explanations because adults are too busy coping with their own reactions to these changing and difficult circumstances.

Not knowing where you live, whose family you belong to or who will be there for you at the end of the day requires constant readjustment and increasing resilience. This resilience can be a thin veil between coping and collapsing, or an impenetrable wall to guard against future hurt. Such multiple transitions in children's home lives can damage forever their capacity to attach to new people and manage new situations, and will make the task of facing a transition in school all the harder to manage.

Children's resilience to new experiences stems, of course, from the experiences they have had in their past. The successfulness of transition, for all of us, lies as much in where we are coming from as where we are going. So, what matters is that teachers take the time to find out what children feel about this transition, and make careful plans accordingly. Some teachers like to talk to children in informal groups. Some like to give them opportunities to write or draw or paint about their feelings. Some ask parents to talk to their child and then to inform staff about the child's feelings – and the parents' own feelings – about transition. Whatever strategy is used, it needs to give teachers robust evidence on which to build their transition programme.

Key principles underpinning an effective transition programme

Figure. 3.1 lists some key principles for effective transition that can inform a school's policy and its strategies for ensuring a seamless journey for children from the Foundation Stage to Key Stage 1.

Figure 3.1 Eight key principles for effective transition from the Foundation Stage to Key Stage 1

1 Transition is a process and not an event.
2 Transition is a whole-school issue.
3 Transition should be viewed as positive and exciting.
4 Transition should be a smooth and seamless journey for all children.
5 Transition should take account of differences and the particular needs of all children.
6 Transition relies on close respectful relationships between families and schools.
7 Transition relies on joint working between staff involved in the process.
8 Effective transition will only be achieved after genuine consultation with children and parents.

---

1 Transition is a process not an event

We have seen that one key principle of transition is that, to be effective, it needs to follow consultation with both children and their parents (see also Principle 8). The outcomes of such consultations should give teachers a strong mandate for setting time aside to prepare everyone for the important move from the Foundation Stage and into Key Stage 1. Those teachers who take transition seriously know that it does not happen on one afternoon in late July! Transition needs planning for, over time, if the needs of all concerned are to be fully met.

One issue that needs to be sorted as soon as possible, therefore, is who will be teaching the classes in September. There is no point in children getting to know a teacher, or a Foundation Stage teacher spending time with a Year 1 colleague, if staff are changed at the last minute and all that effort is wasted. There are some times when this is unavoidable of course. All headteachers know that knock on the door that means a member of staff is coming to say they have successfully applied for a new job, or that they are pregnant, or they have to move house with their partner whose work is taking them away. However, these real-life incidents aside, there are some headteachers who make the decision about staffing at the last moment so that they do not have to confront difficult parents. While it is understandable that decisions about classes and teachers can be challenging, this is not a good enough reason for keeping young children in suspense about who their teacher will be in the new academic year.

Another factor that underpins transition as a process is that one visit is not enough. Children cannot gain the confidence they need from one quick trip to a new classroom. They need a return visit to consolidate what was seen or to see what was missed the first time. All of us know, as adults, that going somewhere new can cause our otherwise efficient brains to freeze with stress and cause us to forget – or simply not 'see' – information that we were anxious to acquire. A young child may be so concerned about where the toilets are on their first visit that they do not look for where their books will be kept or where they will hang their coat. They may be so upset that they have been separated from their best friend that they pay no attention to what the new teacher is telling them about life in their new class. Children, like adults, benefit from returning more than once to a new environment so that anxieties can be erased and so that familiarity brings about confidence.

For example . . .

In one school, children visit to begin with in small groups. They prepare an interview for the Year 1 teacher and video her and the aspects of their new classroom that they like best. Then they share their films with the rest of the class before returning for a whole-class visit later in the term.

2 Transition is a whole-school issue

A second key principle of effective transition is that it is a whole-school issue. This means that headteachers and senior management teams need to understand how important it is for the children – and for the staff – to have time to prepare for transition properly. When we look at some of the strategies adopted by a range of teachers (see Figure 3.2), then we can see that preparation and planning are crucial, and that time and financial resources need to be set aside for the transition to be positive, smooth and seamless.

But, just as important, all senior staff need to understand how children learn when they are in the Foundation Stage and in Key Stage 1. It is no use a Year 1 teacher promoting a play-based approach to learning if the maths coordinator does not understand the maths that is taking place in the sandpit or the block area. It is no use a Year 2 teacher using observations to plan for children's interests and emerging ideas if the science coordinator wants to gather in 'books' to get evidence of children's progress.

Teaching in an environment that encourages and includes child-initiated learning will and *should* look different and be different than teaching in a class of older Key Stage 2 children. Anyone visiting and monitoring a Foundation Stage or Key Stage 1 classroom needs to know, understand and appreciate that. They should be sufficiently knowledgeable to know what high quality learning looks like for their subject when applied to young learners. It is not acceptable that teachers of Key Stage 1 have to use 'whole school' formats and processes if they are not appropriate to the way in which teaching takes place in early primary.

It is not only the monitoring of Key Stage 1 classes that causes teachers concern, but also the inappropriateness of the 'evidence' that some curriculum coordinators require. All staff need to be aware that at 5, 6 and 7 years of age the evidence of children's learning is based on what they *say* and what they *do*. At this age, children's thinking and their understanding is far in advance of their ability to write. If you draw on what a child writes as evidence of what they understand then you may underestimate that child quite substantially. That is why teaching in the early years is so reliant on the *observation* of children's learning. If writing in books was a reliable source of evidence, then Foundation Stage and Year 1 teachers would be carrying home large piles of books to look at and mark – like their Key Stage 2 colleagues. But they do not. Early years teachers are there, in their classrooms, watching and listening to children and recording what they *say* and *do*. From this first-hand and reliable evidence base, assessments are made and planning is created.

In order to ensure that the gathering of evidence is not a mechanistic and tokenistic exercise, curriculum co-coordinators and headteachers should firstly decide what 'evidence' they want. If they want to see progress from books, then the only robust evidence they will see is the development of children's writing. For all other learning, what young children *write* is the least reliable evidence of all.

If headteachers are concerned about 'whole-school-ness' (and some seem obsessed by it) then their concern should be that the whole school understands early learning. In far too many schools, teachers of the youngest children face too many barriers to their practice and pedagogy because ill-informed colleagues do not appreciate the value or relevance of ways of working that they themselves do not employ. Heads need only to look at how many staff meetings are given over to early years practice (in comparison to Key Stage 2) to see that there may be good reasons why some senior staff are not only failing to fulfil their curriculum responsibilities well but are, in addition, creating major hurdles for Foundation Stage and Key Stage 1 colleagues in their pursuit of best practice.

For example . . .

In one school, the headteacher timetabled every Key Stage 2 teacher to visit and spend time observing in the Foundation Stage. A series of staff meetings were then held to discuss what had been seen, and the implications of this for planning, monitoring and school development.

3 Transition should be viewed as positive and exciting

The next principle to underpin effective transition is that it should be viewed as positive and exciting. It is all too easy to forget that, while some children may face change with trepidation, schools must work to make any move onwards and upwards one that is positive and exciting.

First of all this means that, as adults, we should be confident that what children are going to experience is developmentally appropriate for them. Unfortunately we have seen in Chapter 1 that, in many schools, this has not been the case. This is why the majority of this book is concerned with the appropriateness of classroom practice in Key Stage 1. It is no good getting children ready for the move to Year 1, being warm and welcoming as Year 1 teachers if, once the children arrive in class, their learning experiences are alien and unsuitable. Yet it is precisely these concerns that drove teachers across the country to ask their LAs to reconsider 'best practice' in Key Stage 1. We have seen in Chapter 2 that 5-, 6- and 7-year-olds learn by being playful, active and interactive learners. This is the kind of learning on which young children thrive and which harnesses their preferred and most successful strategies.

If children are to view transition as positive and exciting, then so must adults. Adults have to believe that what they are providing for children is drawing on all they know about child development, that it suits their learners and that it suits them as teachers. One tale of caution is from the Year 1 teacher who planned carefully for the visits of children from the Foundation Stage, borrowing resources from her colleagues and making the Year 1 classroom as much like the Foundation Stage as possible. The children were suitably thrilled and full of eager anticipation about their transition, only to arrive in the Year 1 class on the first day of term to find no play resources, a class full of formally set out tables and chairs, and a timetable that gave them no opportunities for self-initiated learning. It was only when the teacher saw the shocked faces and had to deal with several children in tears that she realized that transition does not stop with the visits, but lasts all year through.

Ensuring that transition is viewed as positive and exciting relies on relaxed and confident adults influencing children who, in turn, will hopefully become relaxed and confident. But, as has already been emphasized, that does not mean *assuming* that because the adults are happy about their plans and their efforts to make transition a positive experience, that children will automatically feel the same. Children view the world differently from adults and, while careful planning is crucial, it does not always and necessarily lead to positive outcomes for children. So, we see once again how Principle 8 underpins all others – effective transition can only be planned and evaluated in constant consultation with children and their parents and carers.

4 Transition should be a smooth and seamless journey for all children

There are some teachers who believe that having a transition that emphasizes difference is somehow good for children. They deliberately focus on what is new and different from children's previous experiences – be it in terms of 'proper work' (as opposed to play); 'grown-up behaviour' (i.e. putting your hand up as opposed to making a spontaneous contribution); or meeting targets (i.e. achieving someone else's expectations rather than the child's own). Such emphases are employed so that children are slightly fearful. They are employed to manage children's behaviour and are usually used by teachers who like to remain firmly in control of all that takes place within the classroom.

But such practices will not bring out the best in children. Controlling children is not the way to bring out their most creative ideas, will not encourage them to take risks when they explore and investigate, will not encourage them to believe in themselves as competent learners. Children, like adults, thrive and develop when they feel confident and secure. Certainly there should be rigorous expectations. Certainly there should be experiences that challenge children beyond what they currently know and can do. But that is not the same as creating learning situations that are different in order to put children on their guard. The brain freezes at times of stress. It is alert to the tension and the fear and cannot apply itself to anything beyond those primal emotions. If children are fearful, then they will have no capacity for deep-level learning.

If transition is to be effective then it must build smoothly and seamlessly on good Foundation Stage practice. This does not mean, however, that it will be identical. But it will be sufficiently familiar to give children confidence that they know how learning works in this new Key Stage 1 environment: that they recognize the resources and the way the room is set up; that they recognize the opportunities to play, at times, and the need, at times, to learn from and with adults; that they recognize the opportunities to play alongside their friends and to work sometimes as part of a group selected by the teacher – and so on. All of this familiarity is put in place to make children relaxed and secure, for that is when they will learn most efficiently.

When children are relaxed and secure, *then* they can cope with difference, *then* they can cope with new challenges and expectations. But these differences are not designed to catch children out. They are designed to excite and stimulate children to acquire new insights and learn new skills. They are planned as a result of teachers getting to know their children well and finding out what should be the next steps of their learning. Children will learn new skills and understandings when they are confident in their current abilities, and teachers are aiming to make the transition to Key Stage 1 as smooth and seamless as possible, in order to build on the foundations of children's competent early learning.

For example . . .

One way in which schools are managing this seamless transition very effectively is to establish a 'rolling programme' between Foundation and Year 1 whereby either the teacher or the nursery nurse (or teaching assistant – TA) move up with the Foundation class and take them in Year 1. Then, the following year, the teacher (or nursery nurse or TA) returns to Foundation and the other adult moves on to Year 1. This practice has great strengths, not only in making children's experiences more seamless, but also in ensuring that adults come to know the curriculum well in both key stages.

5 Transition should take account of differences and the particular needs of all children

All teachers know that the children they have in their classes are very different – in terms of their emotional as well as their cognitive needs. Chapter 1 reminded us that a child should not be seen as 'unique' when in

Children in Key Stage 1 need to practise skills they learnt in the Foundation Stage

the Foundation Stage and then as 'a Year 1' when they make the transition to primary education. The 5-year-old who makes that short walk down the school corridor to the Year 1 class needs every bit as much individual attention as he did just six weeks earlier when still in Reception.

We have seen that developmentally appropriate practice means giving children educational experiences that are matched to the stage of their individual development: not grouping children for convenience, but grouping them because they have similar learning needs; not teaching them as one of a whole class if that means that they are either bored (because they understand what is being taught already) or mystified (because what is being taught is beyond their current level of understanding).

So, just as the best teachers plan for the different learning needs of children in their classes, so transition should be planned with those differences in mind. We have been reminded earlier in the chapter that some children are more vulnerable to transition than others – and this may have nothing to do with a child's 'abilities'.

For example . . .

In one school, children who are identified as being the most vulnerable to transition are given additional visits to their new Year 1 classroom. They are given the role of 'class detectives' and they have to report back to their friends in Reception about what they have 'discovered' about life in Year 1. In this way they have a special role which boosts their confidence and they have a 'reason' for their additional visits without being made to feel as though this is a weakness.

For example . . .

In another school, with a number of children with physical disabilities, Year 1 staff are released to have additional training about the needs of their new children before the children arrive in the class. Extra meetings are set up with parents to establish a strong relationship and to have the children's needs carefully explained. The children are given opportunities to visit their new classroom with a chosen friend so they are not overwhelmed by too many other new children, and so the Year 1 teacher has more opportunity to observe how they manage the new space. Together with their friend, they take photographs of what they like about the new classroom to share with their current teacher and with their parents and carers.

All children deserve the best start to new experiences that they can be given. For some this will take more time – and more resources – than for others. But best practice means not assuming that every child's emotional needs can be met homogenously – any more than their cognitive needs will be.

Key Stage 1 children relish first-hand, playful learning experiences

6 Transition relies on close respectful relationships between families and schools

Early education has always emphasized the importance of having close respectful relationships between families and schools. Such relationships matter for all concerned – the child, the teacher and the parent or carer.

For the child, the relationship brings *security* from knowing that special adults at home relate well to special adults in the school. These two worlds dominate young children's existence and if there is conflict or distance between them then this can cause a child uncertainty or distress.

For the teacher, the relationship brings *information* that helps to build a rounded picture of each child in the class. The child that presents themselves at school is not always the same as the child that is known at home. Sometimes the differences between the child known in one world can illuminate what is known about the child in the other. Teachers need to build a close relationship with those at home at the beginning of the child's move into a new class and maintain that relationship all the way through the school year.

For the parent or carer, the relationship brings *confidence* that they are genuine partners in their child's education. It means they are more likely to offer support or help in the classroom or with the child's learning at home. It also means that parents and carers are more likely to express their own concerns or uncertainties about what is happening to their child or about practice in the school.

The key word in relation to this partnership is 'respectful'. In respectful relationships both parties acknowledge that the other has something important and necessary to contribute. It does not mean that one party is dominant. It does not mean that one party is in control. It means that both parties are concerned for and about the child, and that both parties appreciate that together more will be achieved on behalf of the child than would be achieved alone.

When relationships are respectful, then moments of possible tension – such as the move to a new class – can be managed far more effortlessly. The parent feels able to express their own anxieties and/or those of their child. The teacher feels able to ask for advice about how to manage the changes that are to come. Neither party feels threatened and both parties are committed to doing all they can to make the transition successful. When conversations are likely to be difficult they are best managed in a relationship that is already well established and based on mutual trust and respect.

For example . . .

In one school, staff persuaded their headteacher to hold a parents' meeting in June of the year in which children were to transfer, to explain about their new Year 1 learning and teaching plans. The head was reluctant at first – having always held this meeting at the start of the September term. But the staff persuaded her that an early meeting would give parents more opportunity to think about the issues raised – hopefully to be more positive about what their children would experience – and then be in a better position to help their children look forward to their move to Year 1 with eager anticipation.

7 Transition relies on joint working between staff involved in the process

Transition is the responsibility of two sets of staff: those in the Foundation Stage and those in Key Stage 1. We have already seen that there is no point in getting children ready for transition if, when they arrive in Year 1, the teacher does not build on the experiences they have been having in Reception. Likewise, it is of little use the Year 1 teacher trying to plan developmentally appropriate learning experiences for the children if the Foundation teacher is always too busy to share their profiles of the children or to invite the Year 1 teacher into their class to see what the children are currently doing.

Working together can be a new experience for some teachers – even if they have been in the same school for a long time. It is one thing to share news over a lunchtime sandwich and another to discuss pedagogy – and yet this is what is at the heart of the most effective professional relationships and at the heart of effective transition.

Firstly, staff need time to get to know what each person actually does. There can be a lot of assumptions about what practice is like in either key stage. Foundation Stage staff often complain that others think they spend all day 'just playing' and that their work does not have complexity or rigour. Key Stage 1 staff often complain that Foundation Stage staff do not appreciate the pressure they are under to achieve outcomes or to 'get children ready' for Year 2 and Standard Assessment Tests (SATs).

Many barriers can be broken down simply by arranging a series of visits to see what actually does happen and what it means to be a Reception or Year 1 teacher. What such visits may reveal (as we have seen in Chapter 2) is that there are currently differences between practice in the Foundation Stage and Year 1. If so, it is important that these differences are discussed. Are they acceptable differences or will they present problems for children when they transfer?

Once professional relationships are established, a programme of visits can be arranged that focus on particular aspects of teachers' growing knowledge of the other class. Foundation Stage staff (including nursery nurses and TAs) need to visit Year 1 in order to understand what experiences the children will be moving on to. Staff in Year 1 need to visit Foundation in order to see what experiences children are currently having and to start to get to know the children who will be moving into their class.

> ## For example . . .
>
> In one school, the headteacher funded the release of staff to work together on transition for half a day a week for six weeks. This meant that staff could visit each other's classrooms; share records and profiles; do joint observations; and plan – all without having to find time at the end of a busy day.

Increasingly, as Foundation Stage and Key Stage 1 staff work together it becomes apparent that many school issues can be shared. Planning, observations, gathering and moderating evidence are effectively shared when there are good working relationships between Foundation Stage and Key Stage 1 colleagues. Such practices take planning, time and – in some instances – resourcing and so heads need to share the aspirations that teachers have to make transition more effective in order to plan for whatever time and resourcing such initiatives require.

8 Effective transition will only be achieved after genuine consultation with children and parents

This particular principle underpins all the others. It is easy to get carried away with ideas about transition that do not actually meet the needs of the communities we serve. While I have gathered together a whole range of wonderful ideas employed by a range of teachers around the country (see Figure 3.2), these will not necessarily all apply to or be relevant to your children in your current school. In addition, as we have already seen, each idea will not necessarily be appropriate for all of the children in your class. Teachers need to be discriminating: to use what is valuable and to use it only for those children who need it.

Knowing children and their families well will give teachers the starting points for planning an effective programme for transition. Knowing how children and families feel about transition is a whole additional piece of work however. We have already looked at ways in which children can be asked for their feelings about transition, but it is equally important that parents and careers are asked also. They have different views and they can illuminate a teacher's understanding – not only about how their children are feeling, but how *they* are feeling.

Often, previous 'generations' of both children and parents can help inform others about how things really are (rather than how they imagine them to be). But perhaps the most important principle of consultation is that there is no point in doing it unless a school is going to do something with the outcomes. I have become somewhat disappointed by the number of consultations I have witnessed where nothing that is offered or suggested or raised is implemented. These kind of consultations are hollow. The school is paying lip-service to consultation when what they really want to do is just get on with their own ideas. It is all well and good to have your own ideas from the beginning, but if they then exclude anything that is raised by children and families there is little point in wasting everyone's time with a consultation.

However, if schools truly want to improve transition, then consultation is necessary, and responses must be addressed. Staff may not always like what is said – especially if it reflects badly on current practice – but if the aim is to make transition a positive and exciting experience, then schools must be bold enough to listen to the voices of children and their parents.

Strategies to prepare children for the transition to Key Stage 1

In the previous sections there are examples of how different schools have addressed the key principles that underpin effective transition. Over recent years, I have been given countless examples of wonderful practice that individual schools have developed and refined over time. Below, I have selected some of the most effective in order for you to compare these with your current strategies. Maybe, in discussion with your colleagues, you will choose to include some of these in your own planning and preparation for transition.

Figure 3.2 Strategies to prepare children for transition

STRATEGIES FOR STAFF

Reception staff

- Staff consult children and parents about their feelings about the move to Year 1.
- Teacher(s) gives Key Stage 1 staff a briefing about the EYFS Profile outcomes and their implications.

Year 1 staff

- Teacher(s)/nursery nurses/TAs visit Reception class to read stories to children.
- Teacher(s)/nursery nurses/TAs attend any necessary courses about developmentally appropriate practice that builds on the Foundation Stage.

Reception and Year 1 staff

- Visit each other's classes to become familiar with expectations of children and learning experiences of children when they move on.
- Swop classes and teach for an afternoon, a morning, a day, on a regular basis (thus no supply cover required).
- Undertake joint observations of selected children and share possible 'next steps' of learning.
- Meet to pass on information from children's records or profiles, including any knowledge gained from home visits.
- Meet to plan for the long- and medium-term curriculum coverage.
- Move with the children each year on a rolling programme – the Reception teacher becomes the Year 1 teacher and the Year 1 teacher takes Reception (this can also apply to the nursery nurse or TA).

After transition (in September)

- If Reception children do not start at the beginning of term, Reception staff can support any children new to Year 1 who are feeling unsettled over the first few days.
- After a few weeks, Reception teacher(s) visit Year 1 to see whether children are learning according to their expectations and whether children have made the transition positively.
- Foundation Stage and Year 1 staff continue to share and moderate observations of children who have transferred to Year 1.

STRATEGIES FOR CHILDREN

Reception children

- Find out who their teacher is as early as possible (but not so early they become unsettled).
- Visit Year 1 *more than once.*
- Visit Year 1 to work and play alongside buddies (see 'Year 1 children' below).
- Make a book of 'treasured memories' of Foundation to share with Year 1 teacher and/or buddy.
- Take cameras on a visit to Year 1 to capture 'things to look forward to' to share with Foundation teacher and/or parents.
- Draw a picture of themselves on visit to Year 1, so Year 1 teacher can use these to make display to welcome children at the beginning of the September term.
- During visit to Year 1 prepare their coat-peg label/tray label etc. ready for the start of the new term.
- Visit Year 1 in small groups to 'interview' the Year 1 teacher and ask the questions they want to ask (prepared for with the Reception teacher).
- *Those children identified as vulnerable to transition* (see earlier in this chapter) become 'class detectives' who visit Year 1 more frequently and discover more about Year 1 to report back to their class.
- Go on joint outings with Year 1 children.

Year 1 children

- Carefully selected children, currently in Year 1, assigned as 'buddies' to look after/look out for new children making the transition to Year 1.
- Make a PowerPoint presentation of 'things to look forward to in Year 1' and show to Reception class(es).

After transition

- Children visit Reception class in small numbers (if they want to) to share projects or experiences.
- Children have lunch at same time as Reception so as not to face noisy whole-school dinner hall.

- Children accompanied to the lunch hall, to begin with, by a familiar adult (not a dinner lady who has other children to supervise).
- Children feed back on 'things to look forward to' in Year 1, ready for the next cohort of children.

STRATEGIES FOR PARENTS
- Consult with parents about their feelings regarding transition – both before and after the event.
- Hold meeting for parents of children who will make the move to Year 1, to explain the Key Stage 1 approaches to learning (this should be fronted by the headteacher to explain that these approaches are the most effective for young children's learning).
- Hold meeting for parents of new Year 1 children – after the start of the new term – to further explain approaches in Year 1 and see whether there are concerns/queries (the more negative parents are likely to be, the more important it is to hold meetings to allow them to share their concerns – rather than take them 'into the playground').
- Hold workshops for parents new to Key Stage 1 to explain how children's learning needs are met across the curriculum.

Conclusions

The transition of children from the Foundation Stage to Year 1 involves a great many people. It involves time and thought and commitment to ensure that it is a positive experience for all children. It cannot be achieved without wholehearted support from the whole school – particularly senior managers – and it needs to be seen as a shared responsibility between Foundation Stage staff and their Year 1 colleagues.

While the preparation for transition is crucial in its own right, teachers' efforts to make the experience a positive one will amount to nothing if the classroom that awaits the children doesn't build on the principles of effective early learning. The next chapters describe practice in Key Stage 1 classes that is based on the EYFS but that is developmentally appropriate for learners of 5, 6 and 7 years of age.

Things to discuss in your school

- Is transition seen as a whole-school issue?

- Is sufficient time given to the many facets of preparing children for the move to Year 1?

- Is consultation with children – and their parents and carers – at the heart of your programme for transition?

CHAPTER 4

Finding a balance between adult-initiated and child-initiated learning

Introduction

Once teachers agree that 5-, 6- and 7-year-olds learn in highly active and interactive ways, then this can mean a radical rethink of the way in which a day in a Year 1 or Year 2 classroom is organized. We have already seen that the most effective learning environments for this age group are likely to have a balance between learning that is initiated by adults and learning that is initiated by children. But, in recent years, in many Key Stage 1 classrooms, these two kinds of learning have not happened simultaneously. Indeed, in some schools, child-initiated learning has simply not taken place at all. Chapter 2 sets out, unequivocally, the reasons why child-initiated learning is beneficial for Key Stage 1 children, capitalizing, as it does, on their natural and spontaneous urge to find out about and make sense of their world. This chapter reminds us that adults will learn much more about children by observing them engaged in independent, self-driven activities than they will observing them only in adult-led tasks. The chapter will also show why planning a learning day that has child-initiated learning taking place alongside adult-initiated learning optimizes learning opportunities for children. But not only this – a learning day that is balanced between adult-initiated and child-initiated learning also increases opportunities for teachers to give their full attention to high quality, focused teaching in which they can concentrate on the needs of the individual child – alone or within small groups of children learning together.

Working so that children are involved in learning in a variety of ways at the same time inevitably challenges the dominance of whole-class teaching as an effective strategy for learning in Key Stage 1. Since the introduction of the national strategies for literacy and numeracy there has been an increasing dependency on whole-class teaching to deliver some of the most important parts of the curriculum. Yet, when talking to teachers, none of them identified whole-class teaching as the most effective forum in which young children learn.

> When talking to teachers, none of them identified whole-class teaching as the most effective forum in which young children learn.

The following quotes come from the learning logs of teachers involved in the Oxfordshire Transition Project.

'I really despair of whole-class teaching. There are those children who know what I am covering and get fidgety and there are those who are away with the fairies because they simply don't get what I am trying to teach.'

Pat: Year 1 teacher

'I'm never comfortable trying to teach the whole class at the same time. How can I possibly reach all the different needs in my class? The ability span is just too broad.'

Sheila: Year 1 teacher

'Whole-class teaching just seems to waste everyone's time. The children's — because they don't all need the same thing at the same time, and mine — because I know I'll just have to repeat everything again when they go off in small groups.'

Carolyn: Year 1 teacher

Now that many of the more prescriptive teaching strategies of recent years are being challenged and refined, it is a good time for teachers to review when and for what purposes whole-class teaching *is* of value to Key Stage 1 learners.

Whole-class teaching

There is no doubt that coming together as a whole class has value. Children of this age enjoy the sense of 'belonging' to one group and one teacher. There are occasions when a larger group of learners can add to the fun and enjoyment of, say, singing together or hearing a story. There is no better way of enthusing children about a forthcoming project, a visitor or an outing. So, it is important to acknowledge that whole-class teaching has a place in the Key Stage 1 learning day. The box below sums up those aspects of teaching and learning where this grouping seems to teachers to be most valuable.

Whole class teaching is valuable for. . .

- Enthusing the class about a new theme or topic.
- Sharing information about class outings, visits or visitors.
- Sharing singing, poetry, rhymes and stories.
- Quick fun games – phonics, maths, thinking skills.
- Reviewing/sharing work, experiences, ideas.

But having established where whole-class teaching can be valuable, it is important to state where teachers do *not* feel it optimizes opportunities for learning. Drawing on the expert feedback of thousands of Year 1 teachers, it is clear that whole-class teaching is thought to be least effective for activities that require differentiated input or outcomes. In other words, where the teacher is actually teaching – and children learning – at different levels of understanding and ability. In such circumstances, teachers feel their input is far more effective when they group small numbers of children together with others of similar ability. Now it has to be said that not all learning needs to take place in similar ability groups (more on this later), but where differentiation is necessary, desirable and appropriate, then teachers believe that small-group, pair or individual teaching works better than teaching a class as a whole.

Small-group teaching

If small groups are to replace whole-class teaching as the main forum for learning, then this has implications for the way in which the learning day is organized and for the role of the teacher (this will be addressed in detail in Chapter 9).

If the teacher is working with one group of, say, six children, at any one time (if there is no TA) then the majority of the children will, for the majority of their time, be learning independently – in which case, teachers need to spend less time thinking about the group that they are with (teachers are very good at this now), and much more time asking, 'What are the rest of the class doing?'

> Teachers need to spend less time thinking about the group that they are with, and much more time asking, 'What are the rest of the class doing?'

Firstly, teachers have to be confident that children are capable of learning independently. The 'rest of the class' must not be waiting for the teacher to get to them, but should be involved in learning on their own or with peers. This learning must be as worthwhile as the learning that takes place alongside the adult. It must not be see as second-class learning or 'whiling the time away' learning. When children learn independently they learn different things than when a teacher is there. But what they learn can be every bit as important to their learning lives as what they learn with an adult alongside. Adult-led and independent learning draw on different skills and abilities – all of which, when observed by the teacher – give a more rounded view of the child as a learner.

Teachers have to be confident that the learning environment is sufficiently stimulating to entice children to learn. Among other things this means that the environment needs to be set up for the children to find and replace the things they need and to ensure that activities are self-sustaining. Children cannot be independent as learners if they do now know where to find resources or equipment or if they have to wait for an adult to reach something because it is too high or in too awkward a place.

Finally, teachers have to have strategies for interacting with children who *have* been learning independently, to ensure that those children do not feel abandoned. Independent learning is not abandoned learning.

> Independent learning is not abandoned learning.

Teachers should be every bit as interested in what children have learned when they have not been alongside them as when they have. Indeed, I find it all the more intriguing to discover what children have been learning as they have followed their own ideas and interests. What a teacher teaches can lead to very predictable learning – after all, it is planned and the outcomes established before teaching begins. But what happens when children learn more independently, what happens in their minds, what grabs their interest and stimulates their different lines of enquiry, should prove fascinating for anyone interested in how children think and learn.

The benefit of having some children engaged in independent learning while the teacher focuses on a small number of learners is that – when independent learning is of high quality – children will remain engaged in that learning for considerable periods of time, thus leaving the teacher free to teach. In the best managed learning environments, children remain independent learners until the adult chooses to go to them – rather than the teacher being interrupted by children coming to her. A well managed, independent learning environment doesn't have a queue of children waiting to know what to do next.

> A well managed, independent learning environment doesn't have a queue of children waiting to know what to do next.

Small groups and 'covering' the curriculum

Some teachers are concerned about how they will 'cover' the curriculum if children are being taught in small groups. Indeed one reassuring aspect of whole-class teaching is being able to 'cover' the curriculum with some degree of certainty. If certain learning objectives are identified for all, and if the teacher then teaches those objectives, then those objectives can be ticked off as being 'covered'. But is that what teaching is about? Probably not. Teaching is about far more than coverage because what is taught is not always what is learned. In fact, the larger the group of learners and the less differentiated the learning, the less likely it is that an individual child will have learned what was intended.

> Teaching is about far more than coverage because what is taught is not always what is learned.

The way in which many teachers have reconciled this issue is to be honest about how much time individual children are engaged in *learning* (as opposed to 'being taught'). If one monitors the learning opportunities for an individual child over the course of a day then it becomes clear that what is learned as an individual learner or in a small group is frequently far more than what is learned as part of the whole class. Therefore, to begin with, whole-class teaching is often not efficient for the individual learner (only for the individual teacher).

The next issue concerned with coverage is that, frequently, children of this age are kept learning something adult-directed for periods of time that are far too long. At age 5, 6 and 7, children can concentrate for substantial periods of time on learning that is self-initiated but frequently for less time on activities that are adult-led. So, when working with small groups of learners, teachers should make the learning times short and sharp and highly focused, which means that more groups can be taught over the same period of time. In this way children get the same quantity of teaching (in terms of time) but improved quality as well (in terms of differentiated input).

Case study

One teacher I met actually worked out the amount of time an individual child in her class had teaching contact with her in the course of a day. She analysed the quality of that input when her class was largely taught through whole-class teaching and then again when the children were taught in small groups. She was able to convince her headteacher that the quantity of time the children spent with her was roughly the same – but that the quality had increased no end. He was convinced.

Teachers have universally reported that once more small group work is introduced into the learning day, they find that not only does the quality of the children's learning improve – because children are learning in groups of a more manageable size – but the quality of the teaching improves because it is easier to identify what individual children need. It is easier to see when they are struggling to understand. It is easier to see when they rely on others for answers and ideas. It is easier to see how they work things out and go about the business of learning. It is easier to tell if they are switched off and their minds elsewhere.

Should small groups all cover the same aspects of the curriculum?

Although the amount of time teachers spend with individual children when teaching small groups can be seen to be on a par with the amount of time spent when teaching the whole class, and the quality of that time to be improved through small group teaching, there is a further issue regarding covering the curriculum that should alleviate teachers' concerns about how time is spent. When working with small groups, teaching is inevitably more differentiated than in a whole-class situation. As teachers get to know children better they can see that, in fact, not all children need the same teaching every day. There are some children who already know something and merely need an activity that will consolidate their learning. There are other children who struggled with yesterday's concepts and will need reinforcement and reassurance today. There are still other children who need an adult by their side to scaffold their learning and others who will learn what is necessary in a more independent activity or situation.

In other words, in a learner-centred environment, the teacher is not likely to cover exactly the same curriculum in exactly the same way for all groups in the course of a day.

'How much easier teaching adult-focused small groups is. As long as it is well differentiated I can really see the progress children are making and I am more certain that they have learned what was planned. This is just not as easy when teaching the whole class because the range of learning needs is huge. Working in this way also helps me to understand the learning styles of children better.'

Sue: Year 1 teacher

Children learning independently

Working in a classroom that promotes independent learning alongside adult-focused teaching presupposes a belief in the value of children learning without an adult present.

In actual fact, if we monitor the learning experiences of individual children in a classroom where most learning takes place in small groups, in pairs or as individuals, we see that most children will spend most of their day learning independently, rather than with a teacher alongside them.

That is quite a salutary thing to realize because it makes it all the more important that the quality of the independent learning is high and that the teacher believes that learning independently is not a deficit model of learning.

Following a discussion about planning for independent learning, one of the most interesting questions that the Oxfordshire teachers posed themselves was: 'What do the children learn when I am not there?' That is, of course, a very hard question to answer! It required some brave souls to be prepared to have a DVD camera in their classrooms to begin to appreciate what children do when an adult is not by their side. Six teachers agreed to have their children's learning filmed and the outcomes were fascinating.

What children learn when the teacher is not there

- *Social skills:* give and take (children are very strict about rules); taking others' ideas on board; speaking up (or you get left out).

- *Problem-solving:* when there wasn't an adult there with 'the answer' children were more inclined to sort out strategies for themselves.

- *The benefits of trial and error:* children were more likely to abandon things and start again or to take risks and make mistakes if an adult wasn't there.

- *Concentration and perseverance:* if children cared about the activity and were in control of it they were more likely to persevere to a satisfactory conclusion.

Analysis of the DVD material showed not only what children were learning when they were learning independently, but taught the teachers many new things about their own children.

> ## What teachers learned about the children when they were learning without the teacher there
>
> - Children learn *differently* when an adult is not close by. They take more risks, they try out different things.
>
> - Some children are far more *vocal* when an adult is not around. They talk out loud more to their peers and they seem less intimidated about expressing an opinion or challenging someone else's.
>
> - Most children appear to revel in the *independence.* They take control of situations or resources and get 'stuck in' to whatever they have chosen.
>
> - Many children display greater *creativity* and imagination in thinking things through or creating imaginary worlds than the teachers had anticipated. They show skills and competencies that the teachers had not seen when they were close by.

One issue that gave rise to discussion concerned those children who do not revel in independence and those who find 'playing' difficult. The Project teachers discussed children whose culture means that play is undervalued and children whose parents do almost everything for them at home so they lack confidence in making their own decisions. In both cases, the teachers agreed that a parent consultation was desirable in order to share with parents why children 'learning through play' was seen as so important and why children learning independently was such a crucial life skill. Through discussion, it was hoped that teachers could modify their approaches and parents might alter some of the ways they approached learning in the home. In some cases this would be a long and difficult process, but all the teachers believed that when the values and beliefs of home and school were different, they had a responsibility to achieve the greatest synchronization possible.

One thing that interested the teachers was that, as their skills of observation increased, they appreciated that they were learning far more about their children when they observed them learning independently – especially when they were playing – than when they observed adult-led learning. On reflection, perhaps it is easy to see why that is. In an adult-focused activity, the learning intentions are set and, by and large, the children will learn those and the teacher is satisfied. When children learn independently, there is less adult intervention and there are fewer boundaries to the learning. Children cross the artificial barriers between maths and language and design and back again, drawing on skills and understandings in unfettered ways. So, in fact, children have the potential to *learn more* when they are learning independently and particularly, as we will see in Chapter 5, when they are engaged in high quality play: In play: 'a child always behaves beyond his average age and above his daily behaviour' (Vygotsky 1978: 102).

Adult-initiated and child-initiated learning taking place alongside each other

We have seen that in order for small-group teaching to be highly effective, teachers need to ensure that what they plan is based on the analysis of individual children's learning needs. It also depends on the independence of the rest of the class in pursuing different kinds of learning which do not rely on an adult being there all the time.

There are, in fact, three different kinds of learning activities and opportunities that can take place alongside each other in an effective classroom for Key Stage 1 learners. In order for a teacher to focus effectively on one group, she will rely on the quality of the independent learning to give her adequate opportunities to teach.

Different kinds of learning taking place at the same time

1 Adult-focused learning.

2 Adult-initiated learning.

3 Child-initiated learning.

N.B. The word 'adult' is used when describing two of these activities as it may refer to a teacher *or* a TA.

Adult-focused activities

The first type of activity is *adult-focused* (or 'adult-directed' or 'adult-led' – the terminology is not what matters, rather the differences between the nature of these three types of activities). In adult-focused activities the adult has clear learning objectives to achieve by the end of the session. She has pre-selected a group of children who have similar learning needs, and will stay with them until the group has learnt what has been planned. Adult-focused activities are where teachers have most control over learning. The objectives that are set belong to the teacher and – by and large (because teachers are now very skilled at this element of their role) – children will learn what is intended. In order for adult-focused activities to be successful the rest of the class need to be learning independently, so that the adult (and her group) is not interrupted.

Adult-initiated activities

Adult-initiated activities are subtly, but significantly different. They are those activities where the teacher has in mind clear learning intentions but, once the resources are set up and the activity 'kicked off', she leaves the children to learn independently because she is going to work with her adult-focused group.

Adult-initiated experiences focus attention on specific aspects of learning

Adult-initiated activities must, by nature, be different from adult-focused activities, because they will be left to the children to pursue independently and, where children start off in their lines of enquiry may not be where they end up. Adult-initiated learning needs to be:

- sufficiently *clear* for children to be able to work without constantly checking that what they are doing is 'right';
- sufficiently *motivating* that it will sustain the interest and involvement of the children so that they do not interrupt the teacher;
- sufficiently *open-ended* for children to be able to extend it in ways that interest and engage them until the adult comes alongside again (Fisher 2008: 66).

Child-initiated activities

As we have seen, there is a third kind of activity that is vital in Key Stage 1 classrooms if teachers are to capitalize on children's preferred ways of learning at this age. *Child-initiated* activity is vital as a tool for capturing children's enquiring minds and active bodies. It is through such self-propelled learning that young children make sense of their world and come to master new skills.

The place of child-initiated activity, and particularly play, is fully explored in Chapter 5, but suffice to say in this context that child-initiated activities encourage children to make their own choices and decisions about what they will do, the resources and equipment they will use and the processes and outcomes of the experience. *Child-initiated learning is not the same as adult-initiated learning using play resources.* While the latter has value, it does not encourage the creative and imaginative use of children's skills as they pursue their own interests and lines of enquiry. Figure 4.1 shows the balance to be achieved between adult-focused, adult-initiated and child-initiated learning and how each kind of learning depends on the observations and assessments of the teacher to plan them effectively.

Adult-focused learning in more depth

Most teachers are now highly skilled at planning for an adult-focused activity. The benefit of working with small groups of children is that the teacher has assessed the learning needs of the class and is able to bring together children who will benefit on that day from learning a certain concept or skill with the focused support of an adult.

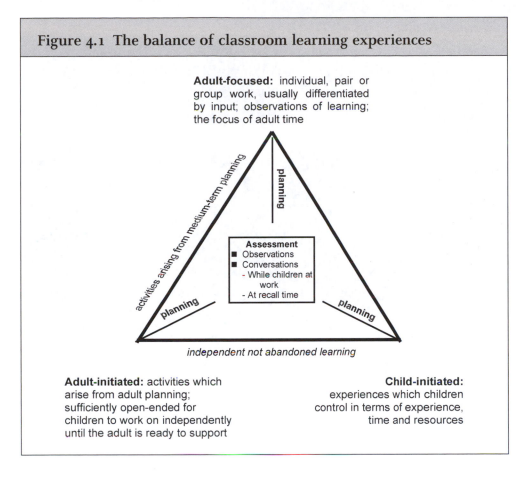

Figure 4.1 The balance of classroom learning experiences

Adult-focused: individual, pair or group work, usually differentiated by input; observations of learning; the focus of adult time

activities arising from medium-term planning

planning

Assessment
■ Observations
■ Conversations
  - While children at work
  - At recall time

planning

planning

independent not abandoned learning

Adult-initiated: activities which arise from adult planning; sufficiently open-ended for children to work on independently until the adult is ready to support

Child-initiated: experiences which children control in terms of experience, time and resources

The children who will work together in this group will not, of course, be the same children on each occasion. The beauty of working in more flexible ways is that a child is not assigned to one group and constantly taught alongside the same children every day. It may be that, for one session, the teacher wants to bring together children of similar ability in order to support them together to achieve a certain objective. But it may be that, on occasion, the teacher wants a mixed-ability group so that children learn different things from working with a wider range of peers.

Whatever the teacher's objective, adult-focused activities will ensure that the teacher can optimize the learning opportunities of a small group of children and can accurately assess their future learning needs.

Adult-initiated learning in more depth

The key to successful adult-initiated activities is their open-endedness. The minute an activity is so tightly prescribed by an adult that there is clearly

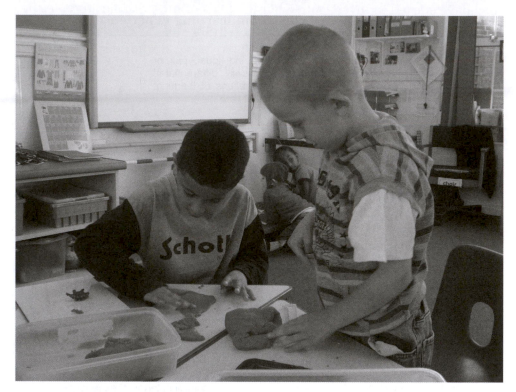

Child-initiated experiences encourage learning without limits

only one way of doing it – and that's the adult's way – children will repeatedly come to check that what they are doing is 'right' or to say 'I've finished'.

But 'planning not to be there' doesn't mean 'planning never to come back'! In other words, independent learning must not feel like abandoned learning. Children soon get a sense of whether a teacher is interested or not in their learning and, while they certainly do not need an adult alongside them every moment, if the teacher just 'leaves them to it' they will soon find other things to interest them – and these may not be on the curriculum. So, once the teacher has finished her adult-focused activity, her next task is to go and see what the rest of the class is doing.

When the teacher goes to observe the adult-initiated learning, one of two things will have happened. Either the children are still completely absorbed in the task, in which case the teacher should observe for a while and then be drawn into the children's conversation to ask questions about their learning or to clarify their thinking (see Chapter 9), or the children may have started to investigate what the teacher intended but then (either because that line of enquiry comes to a natural end or because something has just grabbed their attention), they have gone off on their own tangent and are exploring something quite different.

> 'I decided to put a tray of water with some frogs and a log in the maths area, only to find the frogs returned to their box and the children using the water as a swimming pool for the Mobilo figures!'
>
> *Sameera: Year 1 teacher*

This type of hijacking of teachers' planning can be very nerve-wracking for practitioners who are used to controlling everything their children do and learn. But to be too controlling is to miss countless rich learning opportunities. As long as the learning is still *purposeful* (even though it may have shifted from the teacher's purpose to the children's purpose) then it is still valuable. The teacher needs to wait and observe the direction in which the learning has been taken and then, once again, contribute to the learning with some thoughtful comments or questions to elicit further learning, ideas and understanding (see Chapter 9).

Most things that intrigue and engage Key Stage 1 children are in the National Curriculum somewhere. While it may be that children have gone 'off piste' from the intended learning of the teacher, if they are learning something that has intention for them, then it can be just as valuably observed, assessed and recorded – and used to inform planning for another day.

In summary then, effective adult-initiated activities:

- are open-ended;
- will absorb and interest children until the adult is ready to come back to them;
- often pose problems (that children find worth solving!);
- can sometimes rehearse very familiar skills and ideas (so children know what to do without having to ask);

- can sometimes be an introduction to something completely new (e.g. exploring torches and tents; magnets; lengths of different materials);
- are likely to be hijacked by children's own interests and response to the activity or resources.

Designing effective adult-initiated activities takes a good deal of thought. It is *not* the same as planning an adult-focused activity but with the adult absent. It is worth creating a bank of ideas that work for you and then maybe swapping them with other Key Stage 1 colleagues who may be short of ideas too. Don't forget though, if children are not following your introductory idea when you return to observe their activity, it does not mean that the idea was a bad one (although it might!). Rather, see it as an intriguing example of how children's thinking differs from adults, and how children are likely to become interested in and even fixated on something that the adult would never have predicted.

Examples of adult-initiated activities

Creative development/art and design

Following the story of The Three Bears, the children were given the challenge of designing and making a chair that would take the weight of a given bear (or doll, or dinosaur, or whatever will interest the children most). They had to work in twos and the teacher said she would come back to test their designs later in the session.

Communication, language and literacy/English

A pretend visitor comes to the classroom during the night – a wolf, an owl, whatever will intrigue your children. The visitor writes to the children and leaves the letters in interesting places – both indoors and out. The children write back independently and leave their messages and letters in a designated place.

Problem-solving, reasoning and numeracy/mathematics

Children are given card, pens, pencils, etc. Instructions are to plan a route on a map to find some hidden treasure, or the way to the park, or whatever will interest your children. One child then gives

---

instructions to another child about which directions to take on the map to find whatever is to be found! They then swap.

Knowledge and understanding of the world/science

Children are given boxes of the same size with lids and told their task is to go into the outdoor area and find enough XXXX (dependent on season, e.g. leaves, bark, seeds, cones) to fill the box and on return to the classroom identify them and find out some of their key features (from some judiciously selected resource books). They then plan a quiz for their friends about what they found.

Physical development/physical education

Children are left with a range of 'small skills' equipment (e.g. soft balls, hoops, skittles, etc). Their task is to design, in twos, a circuit of different skills for two other children to complete. The circuit must take at least three minutes – and must be timed.

Child-initiated learning in more depth

Within a balanced model of classroom management, it is vital that child-initiated learning happens alongside more adult-directed and adult-initiated learning. When children are valuably engaged in their own self-propelled activity, a teacher finds herself left with more time to focus on adult-initiated and adult-led learning. Children will remain engaged in play for substantial periods of time, leaving the teacher free to concentrate on small-group, pair or individual teaching.

Unfortunately, over recent years, play has often been used as the 'carrot' to encourage children to finish their work. But this strategy – of play *following* work – has a number of problems. Firstly, it undermines the status of play, in that it says quite clearly that what the teacher is teaching matters most and that play can be given whatever time is left. Secondly, when play is not given sufficient time then it becomes a superficial activity. Play that is crammed into the corners of the day (and the classroom) never has the time to develop quality and depth, and is better off not introduced at all.

One of the most challenging aspects of play is that it can leave adults feeling out of control. If a teacher is used to planning a lesson, teaching it and assessing its learning objectives, then the prospect of observing something that has no learning intentions (other than the private ones of the child), and where the outcomes are unpredictable and idiosyncratic, can be very unnerving.

In this situation, the teacher can often resort to gaining control again. She may do this by planning for learning using play resources – say in a role-play area or an activity utilizing blocks for construction – and then imposing her own adult intentions on the task. We need to be quite clear here that using play resources, but introducing adult intentions, changes an activity to one that is *adult-initiated*. It is *not* play (by the definition given to play in Chapter 5). Play has no adult intentions and no adult outcomes. Using play resources for adult means is not wrong. It can have a valid purpose and a meaningful outcome – but it is not *child-initiated* learning.

Examples of adult-initiated learning as opposed to 'play'

- Children are sent to the role-play area to 'act out' a story from a book. This is a perfectly valid adult-initiated activity but, because it has clear adult purposes and the adult is expecting certain things to be learnt as a result of the children doing it, it is not 'play'.

- The teacher has set up a class 'travel agent'. Here again, there are clear adult intentions behind the activity which the teacher reinforces whenever she joins the children 'in role'. The teacher has spent a long time gathering resources and materials to set the area up. She has planned the language that should arise when children are playing there, the real-life experiences that they will need to draw on to make the play authentic, the visits necessary to give children those experiences etc. But this is not the child's agenda. Often the role-play area is created to support a theme or topic that has been planned to last for half a term, but the children have exhausted the possibilities long before then. In one example a group started to use the class 'garage' to create a stray home for dogs (one child had seen this on the news the night before). The play became multi-faceted and complex as the children used language, problem-solving skills, powers of negotiation and maths to solve the crisis for their imaginary dogs. The learning was significant and entirely driven by the children's interests, but when the teacher joined the group she reminded them that they were 'supposed to be playing at garages'. The children dutifully did so and the activity turned from genuine 'play' to an adult-initiated activity once more.

- The adult hides a selection of letter shapes in the sandpit and the children 'find' them and sort them by some criteria. This activity may use play resources (the letter shapes and the sand) but, with its clear adult intentions, it is not 'play'.

The danger with play in the Key Stage 1 classroom is that it can absorb children so readily that it is easy to 'leave them to it'. But play, just like all other learning that takes place in the classroom, can only be independent for so long, and it must never feel to the children as though their play has been abandoned. Supporting and extending learning through play is a highly skilled business and all Key Stage 1 teachers need to understand that for play to be of high quality it should be supported in just the same way as adult-initiated learning.

So, within the learning environment, adults need to interact with children at play where and when this is appropriate. They must observe the learning that is taking place in play situations and learn about *what* children are learning. Neither adult-initiated learning nor child-initiated learning will survive or thrive without adult support at key moments in the process. In this way, play is supported and develops.

> Neither adult-initiated learning nor child-initiated learning will survive or thrive without adult support at key moments in the process.

If you recognize any of these concerns about the introduction of play and child-initiated learning, then listen to the voices of some Year 1 teachers who, three years ago, were in the same place as you are now.

September

'I really want to go with the children's interests but I'm not sure how to measure the coverage for the children so that I can prove they are doing the same as the children in the Year 1/2 class.'

Chris: Year 1 teacher's log

December

'What a fantastic day, I feel so inspired. As this year is progressing and we are meeting together to share good practice, I am beginning to feel more confident that I can do this. I totally believe now in the Foundation Stage ethos and can see how happy and secure my Year 1 children are. They don't stay in at lunchtimes because they haven't finished their work, they have good self-esteem and their interests are valued. They love school and are learning every day.'

Chris: Year 1 teacher's log

September

'I'm very worried about what my headteacher will say when she comes in to observe [and] I'm still worried about making observations.'

Anna: Year 1 teacher's log

June

'I will look forward to continuing this journey with my new class. I really feel now that I learn alongside them rather than stand at the front and "teach" them. The standards are still good – and parents, children and I are much happier!'

Anna: Year 1 teacher's log

> **September**
>
> 'I am really anxious that the children – and I will not cover everything we have to.'
>
> *Paula: Year 1 teacher*

> **March**
>
> 'The children's play is so rich . . . they learn things I would never have planned for them and I can see I didn't challenge them enough before. It is amazing!'
>
> *Paula: Year 1 teacher*

The balance between the learning experiences of children

As we have now seen, effective Key Stage 1 classrooms have all three types of classroom activity shown in Figure 4.1. But how the balance is maintained *between* these three types of activity will rest with the teacher. It is likely to change according to the age of the children, sometimes from day to day and even session to session. It will certainly change according to the experience and confidence of the teacher.

In the Oxfordshire Transition Project it appeared that as teachers became more confident about play and what could be learned by the children when they were playing, then more time was spent on this and the amount of time on teacher-initiated learning decreased. But this will not happen overnight. You will need to introduce play, observe it and learn from it *before* being confident enough to have it as the foundation of children's learning experiences, and this takes time.

The skill is how to move between the different kinds of activity so that, as the teacher, you feel your time is well spent and – from the children's point of view – you spend enough time with them for them to feel that you are interested in their learning.

The sequence of moving between the three kinds of classroom activity

Whether there is one adult or two within the classroom (see below for a discussion about the desirability of a second adult), the movement of the adult(s) between the three activities can be summarized as follows.

1 The teacher (and/or TA) works with an individual or small group on an *adult-focused* task.

2 The rest of the children are engaged on either *adult-initiated* or *child-initiated* activities.

3 These activities must enable children to be independent of the teacher so that they do not need to interrupt the *adult-focused* task.

4 The teacher completes the *adult-focused* task and moves to both the *adult-initiated* and *child-initiated* activities in order to observe, support or extend these as appropriate (see Chapter 9).

5 Independent learning should not be abandoned learning. Teacher involvement in all activities is crucial if they are to have status and purpose.

6 Once those children working independently have been adequately supported, the teacher returns to the next *adult-focused* activity.

7 The *adult-focused* activity may well be further observation – of, for example, an area of the classroom; the use of certain resources; or an individual child.

8 The rest of the children move independently between *adult-initiated* and *child-initiated* activities until/unless the teacher draws them to an *adult-focused* task (the fewer times children are diverted from child-initiated learning the better).

9 *All* (individual, group- or whole-class) classroom activities are observed and shared at a review time at some point during the day.

How learning and teaching moves 'around' the triangle

One interesting feature of the triangle of learning experiences (see Figure 4.1) in practice is that different activities sit at different points of the triangle on different occasions. For example, the teacher may introduce a mathematical game to a group one day as an adult-focused activity and then, once children have become familiar with the rules of play, it becomes an adult-initiated activity. Equally, the teacher may lead a discussion with a group of children as an adult-focused session before leaving the children to follow up the discussion with an adult-initiated task.

> ### Example of an adult-focused activity leading to an adult-initiated activity
>
> - A teacher had a discussion with her Year 1 class (*adult-focused*) about different ways of 'joining'. The children talked about Sellotape, glue, string, paper fasteners, treasury tags and so on. The next day the children became engaged for long periods of time making houses for the Three Little Pigs using the different materials and testing out different ways of joining them together (*adult-initiated*)

Sometimes, children will have heard a story in an adult-focused session that – several days later – appears in the role-play area as spontaneous play. Conversely, children may engage in block play or water play that reveals to the adult who is observing them that they would benefit from an adult-focused input around a particular skill or area of knowledge or understanding.

> ### Examples of a child-initiated activity leading to an adult-focused activity
>
> - A group of Year 1 children were attempting to make a raft that would sail their 'treasure' to the play 'island' in the middle of the large water tray (*child-initiated*). The teacher observed their efforts and realized that some of the children were uncertain about whether 'heavy things' would sink the boat or whether it was 'large

things'. The next day she planned an *adult-focused* session on floating and sinking, to explore the concepts further with the children.

- Two boys were using magnetic shapes on a whiteboard (*child-initiated*) and discussing whether an isosceles triangle was a 'real' triangle or not. The teacher was tuning in to this conversation and decided to follow up with a group-time session (*adult-focused*) looking at different triangles that would help extend their understanding. *Note: the teacher did not intervene at the time because that would have interrupted the children's flow. The boys were busy constructing a 'transformational machine' and the discussion about triangles was incidental.*

The need for a second adult

Quite clearly, it is easier to operate in this learner-centred way if the class has a full-time TA. Increasingly, headteachers are appreciating that Key Stage 1 classrooms need staffing at the ratios of the Foundation Stage, but this is by no means universal.

In order for schools to earmark funding for increased staffing in Key Stage 1, the first imperative is that headteachers and senior staff understand the role of the 'second adult'. So often there is a misunderstanding that 'second adults' are necessary in classes with younger children because they need support with self-help skills – going to the toilet or doing up shoelaces, for example. But this is very wide of the mark (and certainly not relevant for most Key Stage 1 children). The argument for more adults in Key Stage 1 lies in the fact that children of this age are not able to write at the level at which they are able to think. At 5, 6 and 7 years of age, children's writing is nothing like as advanced as their capacity to understand and to grasp ideas and concepts. If schools rely on what children write as 'evidence' of what they know and can do, then assessments will be based on very shaky ground.

> If schools rely on what children write as 'evidence' of what they know and can do, then assessments will be based on very shaky ground.

What children know and what they can do can only be accurately evidenced by what they say and what they do. This means that evidence of learning and development comes from observation of children 'in action' – it cannot be taken away in books and looked at overnight. It needs to be observed and recorded while children are doing and exploring and talking and trying. Therefore, the more adults there are in the classroom at any time the more observations of learning there can be and the more robust will be the school's evidence of children's attainment and progress.

The TA needs to be someone who works alongside the teacher to prepare the environment, observe the children and offer ideas for planning the curriculum. In order for them to fulfil this role adequately there are certain pointers to the appointment of this significant 'second adult'. A good TA should:

- Be the same person every day and not change mid-week or halfway through the day, as this makes the formation of relationships and any continuity in the children's learning much harder to achieve.

- Begin work half an hour before the start of the school day and finish half an hour after the end of it. This means that she can plan with the teacher, help to prepare the learning environment and then discuss her observations of the children at the end of the day. This has implications for contracts, but it is well worth the planning and effort that it takes.

- Not be whisked off by the headteacher to do first-aid, check the registers, sit with a sick child, run errands – or anything that takes them away from their planned role as 'second adult'.

- Attend training whenever possible to give her an understanding of the principles underpinning a play-based approach so that she does not intervene inappropriately in children's learning, and learns to observe, support and facilitate rather than 'direct'.

- Not be left with the 'younger children' or with 'supporting play' or with 'going outside'. The adults should share responsibilities so that no aspect of the curriculum, no area of the learning environment, no age group or ability group of children should feel as though they are being neglected by their teacher.

With another adult in the classroom there is so much more that can be achieved. One adult can be inside and one can be outside. One can be observing and another can be teaching an adult-focused activity. One can support play while another is working with an individual or group. Both adults can use their eyes, ears and minds to get the best out of the learning environment and the best out of the children. And, as any nursery teacher will tell you, there is a huge advantage in working alongside a knowledge-able and interested second adult in order to share ideas, talk things through and try things out.

'That has been another blessing this week – having my new TA start. It is only early days but it has been much easier working with the same person all week.'

Pat: Year 1 teacher

'Having enough adults makes such a difference. The challenge is in getting the other adult to acknowledge and value child-initiated play. This can only be developed further through time and training.'

Sharna: Year 1 teacher

'I am loving working with my new TA. She is so calm and really perceptive. The classroom is so different from before. We are both trying to do the same thing and that is the best for the children. We have been much more reflective and she stays after school or at lunch to talk through things we've noticed during the day.'

Shona: Year 1 teacher

Conclusions

This chapter has considered the ways in which 5-, 6- and 7-year-olds learn most effectively and the implications of this for classroom management. *Learning* that follows children's own interests, and *teaching* that is tailored to the needs of individual children, are both more likely to be achieved in small groups, or when children are learning in pairs or as individuals. When a teacher spends more time with smaller groups of children the key question to ask is: 'What is the rest of the class doing?' It is imperative that what 'the rest' of the class are learning independently is every bit as worth-while as what they are learning when the teacher is alongside. Independent learning must not be abandoned learning. The teacher needs to be every bit as interested in what the independent learners have been thinking about and trying to do as she is those children who have been by her side. So the skill of the teacher is in giving the same level of attention to adult-focused, adult-initiated and child-initiated activities in order to plan curriculum experiences that draw on the strengths of all those ways of learning.

Things to discuss in your school

- Do children have opportunities for self-initiated learning?

- Does child-initiated learning have the same status as adult-initiated learning?

- Is there an appropriate balance between adult-initiated and child-initiated learning?

CHAPTER 5

The place of play in Key Stage 1 classrooms

Introduction

In recent years the place of play in Key Stage 1 classrooms has diminished. As we have seen, this has been due to misguided assumptions that 'effective' learning is adult-directed and that there is neither space nor time for children to pursue their own self-initiated interests.

Chapter 2 should have shown why such messages are misguided. Effective learning capitalizes on the preferred styles of learners and children aged 5, 6 and 7 are still powerfully driven to play in order to make greater sense of the world around them and to try and test out new skills and understandings in situations over which they have control.

In talking to many Year 1 teachers it is apparent that they have made strenuous attempts to introduce more playful experiences for children, but the issue of control has not generally been resolved. In many Key Stage 1 classrooms play has been 'planned' or 'purposeful' or 'structured' – but, in each case, the planning, the purpose and the structure have belonged to the adult.

However, 'play' is not any activity that is just 'child-initiated', so it is important before we embark on this chapter to establish what is meant by this term. In discussion with Year 1 teachers and after referring to some of the most popular literature on play in early childhood education (see e.g. Bruce 1991; Moyles 1993; Wood and Attfield 2005; Hughes 2009), I would put forward the following features to describe the activity we call 'play'. Play is:

- an activity that is initiated by children using resources selected by them;

- an activity without any intended adult outcomes or any externally imposed processes;

- an activity given time and space so that children can 'wallow' (Tina Bruce's evocative term) in 'ideas, feelings and relationships';

- an activity that is clearly pleasurable and sustains children's interest over considerable periods of time;

- an activity that draws on children's creativity and imagination to develop ideas.

Other authors describe play in their own style, but most who are concerned with early education would include these characteristics within their own descriptions of 'play'. These characteristics are, of course, closely linked to the pedagogy that underpins the development of the learning environments that teachers create for playful learning (see Broadhead 2004; Wood and Attfield 2005), environments that facilitate choice, encourage decision-making and promote collaboration and independence.

For Key Stage 1 teachers, perhaps the most significant of the features of play is 'without any intended adult outcomes or any externally imposed processes'. It is hard to permit such activity in classrooms where someone – be it a headteacher, literacy coordinator, school improvement partner or Ofsted inspector – is requiring that every activity has an 'intended learning outcome'. The moment a playful activity has an intended learning outcome (that is identified by the teacher), it ceases to be play. It becomes, instead, an adult-initiated activity using play resources – valuable in its own right maybe, but not giving children the opportunity to explore, experiment and create in the uninhibited ways that true play offers.

The case for play in Key Stage 1 classrooms

If teachers want to reintroduce play into their classrooms, or to give play more time and space than it has previously enjoyed, then it is important to have a sound rationale to use in discussion with those who may stand in the way of such a goal.

Children want and need to play

The literature about play, and the evidence of our own eyes, tell us that 5- to 7-year-old children still love to play – and still need to play. At this age, play remains a driving force for children discovering about themselves and the world around them. However sophisticated young children may seem in many situations, given open spaces and the most basic of resources they love to involve themselves in fantasy, 'super-hero', imaginative, exploratory play.

This, in its own right, is a good rationale for reintroducing play into Key Stage 1 classrooms. If children want to do it, if they do not need to be coerced or forced or chivvied in order to undertake this kind of learning, then surely teachers should embrace play with open arms. It is rare to hear that a teacher has had to keep a child 'in' at lunchtime to 'finish their play'. Yet how often in transition projects and in reports about transition we hear the plaintive voice of the child saying, 'We used to play in Foundation . . . it was more funner' (Fisher 2009). Over and again we hear how children are grieving for the loss of play and play resources in their more sterile and formal Year 1 classrooms (see e.g. Sanders *et al.* 2005), and we have to question why teachers would elect to remove such a powerful, motivational learning force.

> 'I cannot believe how long the children stayed involved in their play. I thought they would keep coming up to me but they didn't, which just shows that usually they are checking up on what I want them to do.'
>
> *Caroline: Year 1 teacher*

> 'On the first morning I was introducing play I just opened the doors and put some huge cardboard boxes and some large wooden blocks outside and they went wild for a bit and then settled down and the amount of ideas they had were amazing. I just sat back and watched and saw them in a completely different light.'
>
> *Helen: Year 1 teacher*

Through play children will learn many aspects of the Key Stage 1 curriculum

One answer of course is because play is initiated by and follows the intentions of the child, teachers feel they have less control over its outcomes. They feel they have a lot to 'cover' and that they cannot guarantee that children, while they play, will get the curriculum 'covered' in time. This is true. Play is gloriously unpredictable and full of surprises. However, few of those surprises lie outside the core skills and concepts that we will want children to be learning in Year 1 and Year 2. Play is not 'another subject', not something 'other than' the curriculum – it is the way in which most children will access and learn the stuff of the curriculum in a highly effective way.

> Play is not 'another subject', not something 'other than' the curriculum – it is the way in which most children will access and learn the stuff of the curriculum in a highly effective way.

It is true to say that play is less easy to observe and assess than adult-initiated learning. By and large when an adult plans an activity and stays with the children while they are learning what is intended, children learn what is intended. It is predictable and plannable and, although children succeed to varying degrees and at varying speeds, the outcomes of learning are relatively easy to measure.

However, once play is observed over long periods of time, once teachers begin to see the play themes that emerge from different children, once they see the patterns in play and play friendships, then play affords an even richer view of the child as a learner because it encompasses so many different facets of that child.

> 'Reflecting on the play that was observed today, much learning was coming directly from the play. Children were on task and concentrating for large amounts of time. They were being highly imaginative with the resources and this was allowing them to risk-take, an opportunity that doesn't arise much from manufactured environments where most things are fake and plastic and in the control of the teacher.'
>
> *Pat: Year 1 teacher*

> 'Another way to look at this is that there are many skills that can't be successfully *taught*. They need to be learned through the trial and error of play, through the process of finding out how a lid fits on a container or how a key works or how to communicate when you want something achieved as a group. Children are not only fine-tuning their logic, but developing self-esteem and critical social skills.'
>
> *Kate: Year 1 teacher*

> 'Building a race track/obstacle course. This play lasted for about three days. It never ceases to amaze me how well the children work together now. They were nearly all involved in this play, each with their own roles. Their friendships and cooperation has definitely developed over the year and the Reception children are learning greatly from the Year 1s. They are such happy children now, confident in the environment and in who they are.'
>
> *Nadia: Year 1 teacher*

The learning that emerges as children play may be idiosyncratic but it is vibrant and real and often of a very high order and, once the teacher is confident and competent at evaluating it, will provide a rich source of information for planning the rest of the curriculum.

Children remain engaged in play for considerable periods of time

Another rationale for play is that when children are involved and engaged in it, they will concentrate and remain engaged for considerable lengths of time. As teachers, we are always struggling to create quality time to spend with a group of children or an individual who needs our special attention. If the activities we are giving children are done in a flash, if they require explanation and copious instructions, if children spend more time queuing than learning, then there is something wrong with that provision.

High-quality play involves and absorbs children and means that while they are learning alone or alongside other children, then teachers are able to focus on more adult-led learning until ready to observe and join in the play activity.

However, the fact that children can and do play well when alone does not mean that they should be abandoned to do so.

Supporting children's play

Every teacher should spend as much time *observing* play as they do any other learning activity in their classroom. Through observation, teachers will notice skills that a child has, or understandings or theories that they are trying out, that would never be seen in a more adult-directed context. Observation of children at play is a perfectly legitimate *adult-focused* activity but, in order to make the most of observation, teachers have to take time to interpret and understand children's meanings and intentions and not just look for evidence of learning outcomes that are curriculum-focused.

Then adults can *facilitate* play, by introducing resources that might stimulate children's thinking and imagination. These resources might be part of the 'continuous provision' in the classroom – part of the everyday environment that is there for children to return to over and over again as they test out and consolidate their learning (see Chapter 6 for more about 'continuous provision'). However, the teacher also facilitates new experiences – either to 'kick off' a play episode, or to extend the possibilities once a play episode has been going on for some time. This latter contribution is made with great subtlety, because there is a fine line between intervening in children's play and interfering in it.

> There is a fine line between intervening in children's play and interfering in it.

The golden rule of thumb is that if children take no notice of your intervention, then it wasn't a necessary one. Even 'extending' play can seem like a takeover bid to children, and older children in particular are very clear about what the intentions of their play are, and whether an adult is helping or merely getting in the way.

Examples of adults 'getting in the way' of children's play (reports from Oxfordshire Year 1 teachers' logs)

1 'I had put all the small world fairytale characters on a story mat and a group of girls played for a considerable time – firstly creating an imaginary 'world' and then going into character. After about

20 minutes I went across to join in the play and silently, without talking to each other, they picked up the characters and took them somewhere else in the classroom where they continued their storying.'

2 'I had turned the class "shop" back into a home corner to see if this encouraged a greater range of children to come into role play. There were five children playing there sorting out who was cooking and who was going to be the baby. I thought the play needed some direction so I went into the area and asked for a cup of tea. Every single one of the children left and I was left sitting on my own!'

Despite the examples above, adults can become *involved* in play. However, this is a particularly skilled role for the adult – especially where 6- and 7-year-olds are concerned. At this age, as we know, children are becoming increasingly sociable and cooperative in their play and are beginning to develop play themes with their peers and to share an understanding of goals in their play that they have set themselves (see Broadhead 2004 for a fascinating exposition of the social dimensions of play).

As I watch DVD footage of Key Stage 1 children playing and learning together, and the attempts of adults to become involved in children's play, it becomes apparent that as they become 6 and 7 years of age children grow to depend on *other children* for the quality of their play, rather than depending on an adult. This is not to suggest that the adult should never become involved in the play of Key Stage 1 children – but the role changes. The children do not need an 'audience' in the way that they did when they were 3 or 4 years old. They do not need a 'playmate' as often, because they use each other to fill that role. Sometimes they need a helping hand, or someone to fetch something that they are too occupied to fetch, but by and large the adult becomes someone who needs to be *invited* into the play scenario on the children's own terms.

Elizabeth Wood often uses the delightful analogy of the car (the adult) waiting to enter the motorway from the slip-road at just the right moment, so that everyone's journey proceeds smoothly and the cars already on the motorway (the children and their learning) proceed uninterrupted. That explains the role of the adult beautifully. The adult waits for an opening that will not cause the cars already moving at speed to be distracted and to crash. Selecting that moment is very tricky, but one strategy that works for me when I am coming alongside children in their play is not to intervene until they have given me a signal that it is a good time to do so. This signal may be that a child turns to ask a question. It may be that a child invites the adult to hold something or watch something or see something. It may be that the adult is given a role as a character in a role-play scenario. Whatever it is, the 'drivers' on the motorway have 'signalled' that the adult is free to join their lane and make space for them to do so. In this way, the adult is more likely to become *involved* in play rather than *interfere* with it.

This change of role for the teacher can be a difficult one to accept if she is used to being a more dominant figure within the classroom. One of the Oxfordshire Transition Project teachers wrote the following in her learning log.

> 'I used to be the conductor in the middle of the classroom. Everything depended on me and everyone danced to my tune. The biggest change in my practice has come about by removing myself from the centre of the classroom and putting the children there instead.'
>
> *Nadia: Year 1 teacher*

What play does *not* teach

Although play is undoubtedly a necessary way in which children should be learning in Key Stage 1, it is important to stress that it is not the *only* way.

We have seen that high-quality play stimulates new learning, provides opportunities for consolidation and encourages the exploration of many of the major concepts and skills required of both the Foundation Stage curriculum and the National Curriculum. However, there are skills and concepts that 6- and 7-year-olds need to learn that may not spontaneously arise through play.

When I work with Key Stage 1 teachers over a period of time, introducing and observing the power of play in their Year 1 and 2 classrooms, then the inevitable question arises: what does play *not* teach? I now ask this question of any group of Key Stage 1 teachers with whom I work because, if play is to have a central place in the Key Stage 1 classroom, then its status is only truly recognized when teachers say, 'If children will learn X through play, then I do not need to repeat X through adult-focused teaching.'

Play will only cease to be 'another subject' when teachers believe that play and a playful environment teach children certain key skills and concepts (possibly in more effective ways than any adult-initiated activity will) and, therefore, free the teacher to spend their time focusing on those aspects of the curriculum that play does not naturally introduce. While there are occasional differences of opinion (and it will be interesting to know what *you* think), the following is the most universal of lists arising from discussion with hundreds of Key Stage 1 teachers over the past couple of years.

What does play *not* teach?	
Phonics	It is rare for a child to emerge from a home corner saying 'b-b-b-baby' as an outcome of their play. Phonological awareness needs regular small-group teaching to be relevant and purposeful.
Handwriting	Although play is the most powerful route to children writing for a range of purposes (lists in the shop, appointments by the phone, charts for the bikes outside, etc.) handwriting practice needs to be under careful adult supervision in a small group.
Calculating	Although play provides a wealth of opportunities for developing concepts about space and shape, measures and counting, the opportunities for understanding and developing calculation strategies are more limited and need adult-focused teaching.
Place value	Similarly place value, not a concept that naturally seems to arise in play and hence needs adult-directed teaching.
RE	While many of the values about respecting others and their ideas, values and beliefs arise very spontaneously as children play together (and are understood more meaningfully in this kind of environment rather than one that is adult-controlled) the *facts* about different religions and different cultures do not

	always arise in play situations and have to be taught more explicitly.
Skills	A number of skills, from across the curriculum – such as cutting and joining, logging off a computer, backward rolls, and throwing and catching; were identified by teachers as arising in play but needing adult support and intervention at the right time to be taught correctly in order for children to be safe and skilful.

Play and more able learners

One belief about play provision that I have noted in discussions with teachers in Key Stage 1 is that play is necessary in classrooms only for younger or less able children – for those who are not yet developmentally mature and 'ready' for the more formal learning that can characterize the Year 1 curriculum. It is really important that we report quite different findings from the Oxfordshire Transition Project. The teachers' learning logs, as well as the evidence from the DVD footage, reveal that in Year 1 and Year 2 classes play is often at its most powerful and effective as a vehicle for learning for the *most* able.

> Play is often at its most powerful and effective as a vehicle for learning for the *most* able.

Time and again I have observed groups or pairs of very able children engaged in play that has shown them working beyond what had been perceived to be their capabilities. In play there is no imposed ceiling on what a child shows that they know or can do. On the other hand, in an adult-initiated activity, the child is working within the parameters of the given task. The teacher teaches the child X and – by and large – they learn X. That learning may be at a higher level of understanding than other children in the class, but the outcomes are still constrained by the limits of what the teacher has planned for the child to learn. In play, no one gives boundaries to the learning, so children explore at the very edges of their own experience, reasoning and imagination.

'Play seems to be as important for the more able. My boys definitely fit this category. Their play and ideas for play are more sophisticated . . . They access the classroom independently and know that what they do is valued instead of being told what to learn and being given a worksheet/activity to complete.'

Sue: Year 1 teacher

The following is an extract from a DVD transcript of five very able Year 1 girls who spent over an hour building a 'bus shelter' from the construction material 'Quadro'.

G1:   Rachel are you sure it's not going to fall?

G2:   No!

G3:   Rachel, Rachel.

G4:   Down down. It's broken.

G5:   We need to go down so we can put it on the floor.

G3:   Rachel, Rachel you're breaking it.

T: Do you need some more?

G3:   Oh you're breaking it again Rachel. Now look it's broke.

G2:   How is it breaked?

G5:   Look it's breaking down the bottom there.

G3:   Rachel . . . Rachel stop bending it it's too high.

G2:   Oh it's ginornmous.

G5:   I know . . .

G1:   It's not supposed to be so tall or it will fall.

G5:   We need it to attach it there.

G3:   Ohhh, Rachel!!

G5:   We need that . . . we need this there.

G3:   Rachel! You're making it break.

G4:   No, we need to come up this end too so it's even.

G5:   No but then we have to break this bit to make it even.

G3:   Be careful!

G1:   Can somebody hold this bit?

T: I will.

G3:   Rachel, hurry up.

G4:   Can somebody put the block here to even it up . . . On the top.

T: Am I in your way?

G2:   Yes we have to move this.

G5:   It has to attach.

G4:   No look that's going up that one and we need it to go that way.

G5:   We can't have it there it's not even.

G4:   Yes, yes it's all right.

G5:   We need to take that bit off.

G1:   We need to take the green bit off.

G4:   Break that bit off . . . Make it a bit shorter.

G1:   Shall we leave the bricks til afterwards?

G2:   Yes the bricks.

T: You need to build this side up possibly?

G1:   We need to take this top bit up.

G2:   Take that off.

G1:   Right that's that one off.

G4:   This one's in place. Right.

G2:   We're going to do this for ages.

G1:   One, two, three, four, five, sux, seven, eight, nine, ten, eleven. Eleven squares.

G4:   We need . . . we got seven. Four more.

G2:   My sister's eleven.

G1:   My sister's nine.

G2:   My sister's ten.

G3:   Oh. My sister's ten and annoying. Mrs Smith my sister's ten and annoying.

G5:   We need a connector.

G1:   We've got eight. Nine, ten, eleven . . . three more. We've got nine we need three more.

G3:   Two. I've already got two.

G4:   One to go across the middle.

G5:   We need a connector.

G1:   Nine, ten.

G5:   We need a connector. A connector.

G2:   We need a connector.

G4:   It's breaking.

G1:   Oh it's breaking.

G5:   We need a connector.

G4:   A connector.

G1:   Six, seven, eight, nine, we need two more.

G2:   It's wobbling.

G4:   Is this our last one?

G2:	It's wobbling.
G3:	Rachel, Rachel.
G2:	One of the bricks is falling down.
G5:	Now what? What do we still need?
G4:	We need a connector on that one and a brick.
G2:	We need a connector.
G5:	A connector up there.
T:	What do we need now?
G3:	'S'going to be hard to take it down.
G4:	Another connector right.
G5:	I'll hold this end.
G1:	Connector.
G2:	Connector.
G3:	We need Sophie to hold it now.
G1:	There we go.
G5:	I'm just fixing it down the bottom.
G4:	You're breaking it.
G5:	No I'm fixing it down the bottom.
G4:	We need some to go down here.
G3:	Ahhh.
G2:	It's breaking.
G4:	Ahhhh.
G5:	We need to go across.
G4:	There's too many people.
G5:	Hold it at the bottom.
G1:	It's too wobbly.
G5:	I think it's too high. It's too high.
G4:	Get under the shelter, maybe three.
G5:	Only three people allowed, only three people under the shelter.
G4:	Everyone it's breaking at the bottom.
G3:	Oh no all of it.
G2:	This is funny.
G4:	It isn't funny.
G3:	There's too many people.
G4:	It's wobbling.
G2:	Ohhh.
G1:	Ahhh.
G3:	Oh oh.

The structure collapses

This extract shows how complex the children's thinking is, how much they have to draw on their powers of negotiation, how they struggle to manage different members of the group with different skills, how much they are challenged by their existing knowledge and understanding of buildings, materials and construction techniques in achieving their desired goal.

It is so important that, if children are more able, and if they show that they are ready for more formal skills and advanced thinking, that we do not 'reward' them by constraining their learning experiences to what is written, static and adult-directed. In addition, just because a child is able – in terms of literacy, for example – it does not follow that they have well developed social skills. One teacher reported that her able autumn-born girls – those who regularly sat at the front of the class carpet with their hands up – simply could not manage the cut-and-thrust of more independent learning. They squabbled and sulked and needed support to learn to live with and play with others positively and effectively.

One of the great assets of playing together – and being independent of adults – is that children learn the social skills needed in situations that a teacher might sanitize too quickly.

> Playing together . . . children learn the social skills that a teacher might sanitize too quickly

For example, when children play together they have to learn to put forward their own ideas and sometimes have them rejected; they have to learn to listen to the ideas of others and go along with them even if it isn't their preferred option; they need to learn to argue their corner, to be more assertive, to compromise and to cooperate. If, in a teacher-led situation, children were to start on the kind of interactions that you often hear as they play together – the squabbling, sometimes the use of bad language, the attitudes and the recriminations – then the teacher would probably step in to try and smooth things over. But in these real-life play situations, the skills of collaboration and cooperation are more genuinely learned than in, say, a whole-class circle time when 'being nice to others' is the topic for a decontextualized debate.

Play and 'standards'

It is important to address the 'standards' issue. During my inservice sessions with headteachers and teachers I have heard, frequently expressed, the fear that allowing children to play will somehow depress standards.

This appears to link with a notion that playing is really 'playing about' and that nothing serious or necessary comes from play, only from adult-initiated learning. I hope the preceding paragraphs have helped to counter that argument effectively.

These concerns also suggest a view that children only learn effectively when an adult is present. That children, as they are playing, are somehow only 'marking time' until they can go and work alongside an adult. This too is a myth, and hopefully Chapter 4 will have helped to dispel such misunderstandings. The experience of the schools in the Oxfordshire Transition Project and, indeed, in other LAs where high quality play has become a central process for learning in Key Stage 1, is that standards – in many aspects of the curriculum – have been raised.

> Where high quality play has become a central process for learning in Key Stage 1 . . . standards in many aspects of the curriculum have been raised.

If teachers base their practice on the developmental needs and interests of the children in their class, then it is logical that children's learning will benefit as a result. Not only that, but children's attitudes and approaches to their learning will be improved.

Why standards are likely to rise in learner-centred classrooms

- Having more opportunities to initiate their own learning gives children a greater stake in their education. It enhances their self-esteem and self-confidence and gives them a vested interest in how they go about the business of learning. They are more likely to settle to adult-focused activities when they know that a substantial part of their day is in their own hands. Improved attitudes to learning are motivating. Motivation increases children's self-confidence and, as research shows, this in turn can enhance children's educational outcomes (Dweck 1978). In the Oxfordshire Transition Project there was a significant improvement in children's attitudes to learning.

- Play gives children greater opportunities to be together for a purpose, to talk together, to reason and argue and put forward a point of view. In this way, children become more confident to speak out and to have an opinion, feel more ownership of the talk and its outcomes and generally improve their skills of speaking and listening. In the Oxfordshire Transition Project there was a rise in standards (in teacher assessment at the end of Year 1) in speaking and listening.

- Play opens up many possibilities for children to write for a range of purposes. Children seem to respond to writing when they are not required to write in decontextualized situations at a table. Boys, in particular, do not seem to like writing in books so teachers tried clipboards and pencils; whiteboards and marker pens; scraps of paper for making lists; card for making invitations; chalkboards for organizing wheeled toys outside . . . any and every opportunity for writing to be a purposeful part of an activity rather than something separate and possibly more intimidating.

- Almost every teacher participating in the Project who introduced play as a major element of the learning day said that standards in writing had improved – especially for reluctant writers. The Project did not set out to do this in particular, but it is salutary to note that by removing the emphasis on the formal, adult-led teaching style so prevalent in recent years, the quality of children's writing generally improved. This is not to say that there was no teacher-led writing in the Year 1 classrooms. But when this occurred, children had had a wider range of writing experiences at which they were successful and where they had been prepared to 'have a go' because the results (in terms of bits of paper, whiteboards etc.) were transitory. In the Project there was a rise in standards (in teacher assessment at the end of Year 1) in the writing of less able children.

Play offers opportunities for investigation, creativity and writing for a purpose

Introducing play into a Key Stage 1 classroom

Very often, for teachers who are not used to planning for or using play as a learning strategy, getting going can be the hardest step to take. The important thing to remember is that high-quality play does not materialize overnight. Even experienced teachers find they have to try out resources, reorganize the classroom space, and learn when and how to intervene over a considerable period of time before they feel that what they are providing for their children brings about play that is rich in learning potential.

In the current educational climate it is difficult to argue for time for the *adult* to 'play', because there is such an emphasis on planned outcomes – and the results have to be immediate and visible 'now'. This outcomes culture is, of course, anathema to creative and developmental teaching. All good teachers know that to become good takes time, trial and error. If teachers are not allowed periods of trial and error then there will be no growth. Teaching will remain safe and predictable and no one will have the courage to try things out that might initially go wrong.

> If teachers are not allowed periods of trial and error then there will be no growth. Teaching will remain safe and predictable and no one will have the courage to try things out that might initially go wrong.

Only from experimentation – and mistakes – comes innovation. Children's experiences will become more and more routine and repetitious if schools insist on repeating the same format – even when it is not always satisfactory or maximizing children's learning potential. In order to develop their own practice, teachers need to be given permission to introduce play, even if it takes time to develop the rules, the structures and the environments that sustain play of high quality. Poor quality play is usually caused by the misunderstandings of adults. Some examples are given in the following sections.

Children are given opportunities to 'play' on one afternoon a week

So-called 'golden time' will never develop play of high quality. When play is kept as something special – rather than a key way in which children learn – then play is seen only as a 'carrot' for getting finished the more important teacher's work. Play has so much more value than this and needs to be utilized so that children learn science and creativity and geography and personal development as these, and other, core skills and understandings naturally and spontaneously arise in play scenarios.

In addition, 'golden time' means that children don't see play as a central part of their everyday learning opportunities. They are more likely to get over-excited when the lid is taken off the teacher-dominated agenda and they have the chance to follow their own interests. Teachers very often report to me that behaviour during 'golden time' is very poor, that children are very loud and over-excited. This stands to reason. If children are deprived of something, they get over-excited when they *can* have it. The fact that children anticipate and are 'allowed' to have fun for a short period of time means that – just like at birthday parties – behaviour gets hyped up and the quality of the play actually deteriorates.

Children don't have long enough in the day to develop play that is of good quality

If you talk to most early childhood specialists they will say that *good quality* play doesn't often emerge from the start of a play episode. This is supported by Broadhead's research (2004) which demonstrates that children need time for play to develop in social complexity, and to result in more challenging social and cognitive outcomes. It can often take around 30–40 minutes for children to become completely immersed in their play and to find something that they want to create or to pursue. At the beginning of play episodes children are more likely to 'play around with' materials and resources (especially if they are not familiar with them). Then they are likely to play around with ideas and possibilities while they find something that appeals to them. All the while they are likely to be talking to, arguing with and negotiating with, the friends with whom they are playing in order to settle on something that interests them all. All of this takes time. If children are only given 10 minutes before lunchtime, or 20 minutes within a 'carousel' of activities before they are moved on, then play will never develop beyond the superficial 'playing around' stage. Of course, there are times when children who are used to playing together can pick up a well-loved play theme and get into their play more quickly. There are also times when play resources are so well known and used – such as

Play should be absorbing and engage children's attention

Lego or water – that play develops more quickly. But often, the kind of play that draws on new ideas, that involves exploring the possibilities of new resources, that demands the most innovative and imaginative ideas – takes time to develop and must be given time if it is to be of the quality that makes it worthy of a constant place in the classroom.

Resources are inadequate to support the play that children want to engage in

Very often when I speak to Key Stage 1 teachers they complain that they do not have the level of resourcing that is enjoyed by teachers in the Foundation Stage. They feel they cannot introduce play of good quality because their resources are simply not adequate. While it is true that money needs to be invested in a play-based learning environment (see Chapter 6 for ideas and suggestions) it is reassuring to note that many of the resources that appeal to resourceful, imaginative 5- to 7-year-olds are completely free! Many of the Oxfordshire Transition Project teachers were won over by their children's creative response to large cardboard boxes (from the purchase of fridges or freezers for example); empty shoe boxes; old plastic milk crates; pieces of material from ends of rolls; the inserts to rolls of carpets, etc. More important than money is teacher ingenuity and imagination. Teachers need to see the playful possibilities in everyday things, gather them up and try them out.

In contrast to the dearth of high-quality play resources in many Key Stage 1 classes, I often see too many beautiful role-play areas. I must explain that I have nothing against role play – indeed it is an incredibly valuable feature of a play-based learning environment. But the problem comes when the role play is hijacked for the teacher's intentions. The class is following a topic on, say, 'People Who Help Us', and so there is a role-play area that is a hospital, or a doctor's surgery, or a fire station, or a police station. Very often teachers spend an inordinate amount of time developing these role-play areas so that children can gain as much learning from them as possible. Children go on visits to the 'real thing' (hopefully). They have visits from the 'People Who really Do Help Us' – a firefighter or a police officer comes to talk to the class. Resources are vigorously gathered together. Signs and labels are meticulously prepared. This can take a very long time and a great deal of teacher energy. If the role-play area is introduced well and the teacher and TA model the various 'roles' that can be played, then the area is often very popular to begin with. But children do not tend to stay with the same play themes for very long – especially when the theme is not their own, but one that was introduced by the teacher. Left in the hands of the children, the 'doctor's surgery' transforms into . . . a vet's surgery (because one child's hamster has been taken to the vet the previous evening); a hotel for dogs (because several children saw a programme about that on television); a pirate's lair (because a child watched Johnny Depp one evening); or 'my granny's house' (because one child wanted to re-enact a favourite personal story). Now, at this point a teacher has a choice. She can say, 'Well this is what is interesting the children so I will let them run with this interest and go with them.' Or she might think, 'I put a lot of time and thought into this doctor's surgery / fire station / travel agency; I want the children to learn the language of the fire station or the travel agent; I want them to know what it's like to be in the role of the visitor who came into the classroom; I spent a lot of time creating this space and I want them to play with it for longer.' In which case the play possibilities are dictated by the teacher and – by the definition we used at the beginning of this chapter – the activity ceases to be play in its truest sense and becomes an adult-initiated activity because it is underpinned so clearly by adult intentions. Once again, I emphasize that there is nothing wrong with an adult-initiated activity that uses playful resources – far from it. But such an activity shouldn't be confused with play and, as role play is the type of 'play' that has frequently survived in Key Stage 1 classrooms, it is doubly important to clarify what kind of learning is really going on and that this kind of role play is no substitute for free-flow, child-initiated play.

Teachers don't observe play often enough to have evidence of children learning

A further barrier to the development of good-quality play is that teachers do not observe it often enough to have evidence that it is worthwhile. When you have not experienced something, it is difficult to believe that it has the worth that others suggest. Many teachers will talk – in interviews if nowhere else – about the value of play and its place in the classroom, but in reality play is assigned to the edges of children's learning, given adult outcomes (see above) or not introduced at all. If the theory about how children learn and your own experience of children playing outside the school environment, or in the Foundation Stage, has given you a glimmer of understanding that play is something worth exploring further, then you just need to start . . . and see what happens.

The teachers in the Oxfordshire Project were amazed at the levels of their children's involvement and engagement in the play opportunities that they introduced. Although the quality of the play wasn't necessarily good from the beginning – indeed, in most cases it was not good from the beginning – there were enough glimpses of what could develop for the teachers to persevere. With the introduction of play, however, must come the introduction of observation (see Chapter 7). Play is not there to while away children's time happily or to keep the children out of the teacher's hair while she gets on with something more valuable. Play, as we have seen, offers children learning opportunities that more directed adult teaching can never do, and teachers must make time to find out what those are.

Once play is observed regularly, teachers begin to see the learning taking place. They begin to see things about individual children that they hadn't seen when they were learning in more formal situations. They see competences, characteristics and dispositions that do not emerge when an adult is directing the learning. They begin to see how the organization of the learning environment impacts on the quality of what children are doing. All of this invaluable information is then fed back into planning for the next steps of children's learning and gives the teacher a heightened resolve to continue with play in their classroom – and to improve it.

Teachers abandon children's play, so they do not learn how to intervene to enhance its quality

As I suggested earlier, intervening in children's play can be fraught with dangers. It is all too easy to say the wrong thing at the wrong time (we've all done it) and to stop the play dead in its tracks.

> It is all too easy to say the wrong thing at the wrong time . . . and to stop the play dead in its tracks.

If a teacher has not understood what is motivating her children's play, if she has not taken the time to understand what the children are trying to achieve, then it can mean that any intervention will be ill-judged and, far from extending children's thinking and learning, it will interfere with it.

Children have their own learning momentum. If they are deeply engaged in a play episode they will have their own intentions and their own goals. If the teacher does not tune into these, then any intervention will hinder learning and not help it. Observation is the key to good intervention. Knowing when to step in – indeed, *whether* to step in – relies on having tuned in to what children are thinking and trying to do. This does not mean never engaging with children's play at all for fear of getting it wrong. Experience – and experiences – teach us all to be more skilful at suggesting something, introducing something that takes play to new levels. But unless we develop our role in the ways described earlier in the chapter (and in Chapter 9), children will see play as less important in the eyes of the teacher because the teacher never stops by to see what is happening.

Steps to introducing play into the Key Stage 1 classroom

1 Gather open-ended play resources that children can use for their own creative ideas (if you're not sure where to start, go and look at a good Foundation Stage class).

2 Give play time and space in the classroom. Don't interrupt it with any adult-led teaching and see what happens. (Inevitably there will be times when children's play is interrupted but it is important to understand what can be achieved when it is not; this will inspire you to plan a learning day that leaves children with long periods of sustained learning through play – see Chapter 8.)

3 Once a play episode has established itself, go and observe to see what children are learning. Don't interfere unless children invite you in.

4 Use what you have learned through observation to plan for further play opportunities *and* for adult-led learning

5 Go on courses about play, read about play, go and see play in good nursery and Foundation Stage environments.

6 Use what you have learned to improve your skills in supporting, extending and providing for play.

Conclusions

The place of play in Key Stage 1 should now be assured. We have seen that it is one of the most powerful and motivating ways in which children age 5 to 7 learn, a view supported in the final report of the *The Independent Review of the Primary Curriculum* (DCSF 2009: para. 4.49):

> Play is not a trivial pursuit. Drawing on a robust evidence base, the interim report highlighted the importance of learning through play . . . The purposes of play in promoting learning and development should be made explicit and planned opportunities made to fulfil them in the primary curriculum.

However, for play to be of the quality necessary to be given classroom space (on the timetable as well as in the room) it must be given the time and attention it deserves – both by children and by teachers. Children need time to develop play that has depth and that has purpose. Teachers need time to observe and extend the play through carefully judged interventions – be they verbal or physical. The most important message is that without play in Key Stage 1 classes, teachers will only ever see one facet of their children's learning. With opportunities to follow their own interests and manage their own outcomes, many children will show that they have far more potential than may previously have been recognized or appreciated.

Things to discuss in your school

- What is your own definition of play? Does it involve children's intended outcomes or teachers'?
- Do you observe play often enough to have evidence of children's learning?
- Are children engaged in play of high quality? If not, what might you need to improve in your provision for play?

6

Environments that support different ways of learning

Introduction

When teachers work with small groups of children, with pairs or with individuals, it means that, for the majority of their day, most children will be learning independently. If the teacher is alone in the class, without TA support, then up to six children at any one time might be working with the teacher while the remaining 24 or so are alone or alongside their peers. This is why it is so important that children's independent learning is seen as every bit as worthwhile as learning that takes place alongside an adult.

Much of children's independent learning will be stimulated and sustained by the learning environment that surrounds them. Sustained – in that children are *enabled* to be independent – stimulated – in that children are *encouraged* to be independent.

Sustaining children's independence

When teachers want to improve the quality of children's independent learning, then the learning environment must be organized to support this so that children's independence is *sustained*. This requires that teachers consider the way in which they organize both space and resources.

Space

We have seen that children in Key Stage 1 learn most effectively when they engage in playful, active learning. So it is crucial that their classroom environments are designed to promote this way of learning. Most importantly, active learning requires space. Many children, moving from the

Foundation Stage to Year 1, comment on the lack of space and, indeed, many Year 1 teachers complain that there isn't room for play resources alongside their more traditional classroom equipment and provision. Creating the right spaces for active learning frequently demands a fresh look at current provision to see whether the way a classroom is organized actually promotes the kind of learning that the teacher desires.

Sufficient space

The best way to create more space for active learning is to have an outdoor learning environment (see more detail about planning for the outdoors below). Once a school creates outside learning areas for its Key Stage 1 children the first thing that is commented on is that there is so much more space for learning indoors too. This is one of the main reasons why children's behaviour very often improves. When you are not bumping into tables or squeezing past your friends, when there is more space for resources to be set out and when there is less need to share cramped spaces, then everyone can relax more and there are fewer incidences of conflict.

However, when classroom space is cramped, the first thing to do is to take a long hard look at the number of tables and chairs that fill that space. Tables and chairs restrict the amount of space that is available for children to learn in different ways and also restrict the flexibility of that space to be altered to suit the activity that is going on.

> Tables and chairs restrict the amount of space that is available for children to learn . . . and also restrict the flexibility of that space.

It is simply not necessary for every child to have their own table and chair. Sometimes, a table and chair for every child is provided to give children security – 'their' place; 'their' belongings. My experience – and now that of many Key Stage 1 teachers, is that as long as children have a place of some kind such as a peg or a drawer with their name on, then that is quite sufficient.

Sometimes, every child is given a table and chair as a controlling mechanism – making sure there is one chair for every bottom can make some teachers feel more secure. But in an active, play-based environment there is less need for the teacher to 'control' things. Children are engaged more frequently in activities that interest and engage them and they are less likely to need 'controlling'. One frequent comment from Year 1 teachers has been that since introducing a more play-based approach children's behaviour has improved exponentially.

> 'As the quality of play improved in my classroom, so did the children's behaviour.'
>
> *Pat: Year 1 teacher*

Sometimes teachers say, 'I like to have the whole class together for hand-writing or for story writing.' Having explored the developmental needs of Key Stage 1 learners (in Chapter 2) it soon becomes apparent that this is ineffectual use of time. As we saw in Chapter 4, having the whole class together may mean that everyone is *covering* the same thing at the same time, but it does not mean they are all *learning* effectively at the same time. If children need to learn such demanding skills as handwriting or such creative skills as story-writing, then most teachers prefer to do this with smaller groups where they can concentrate on the very different needs and abilities of the children in their particular class.

So, classroom space needs to provide the best opportunities for active learning, and tables and chairs just get in the way. Some very bold Year 1 teachers that I know have started by removing every table and chair in the classroom (having negotiated this with the caretaker of course!). Then, as the children learned to use the space for independent, playful activity, the teachers (and children) could see where tables were needed and wanted. So, in some classes, children said they wanted a craft and design table constantly available – with all the materials to make and create close at hand. In another class, the children wanted a table for writing (although in many classes children seemed to prefer to have a table for the writing *utensils* – and to actually write anywhere that *wasn't* a table). In one class, the children preferred a table for their small-world play. Every class will vary, but the core principle is that tables take up space and so every table must have a use – or it should go.

Flexible space

Whatever stays in the space to encourage children's independent learning must remain sufficiently flexible to respond to whatever learning the children are engaged in. On some days, playful exploration can extend across a whole classroom and so it matters that there is nothing in the way to inhibit the pursuit of children's interests and endeavours. Purchasing furniture that can be wheeled and moved easily, thinking through the use of carpet space – having one space for whole-group times and one where construction or small-world play can continue without being 'packed away' – help the environment to sustain the level of independent learning that Key Stage 1 children need and enjoy.

Spaces for different kinds of learning

There is a need – both indoors and outdoors – to recognize the breadth of learning opportunities that children should enjoy as part of their daily learning experience. There need to be:

- quiet spaces *and* places for action;
- spaces for individuals, for small groups *and* for larger groups;
- spaces to be alongside an adult *and* spaces to be learning alone.

But in any one classroom there is not only a need for different kinds of learning spaces, there is also a need to plan for the needs of different kinds of learners. Children will vary considerably in their preference for working with others or alone; for being tucked away in a corner or in the centre of things; near an adult or a long way away. These preferences may vary from day to day and mood to mood, but this consideration of 'difference' reminds us that any classroom that announces 'There is only way of learning here' cannot be meeting this range of needs and is unlikely to appeal to all its learners. So, returning to the 'tables and chairs' theme, the classroom that, every day on entry, has 30 tables and chairs and a stack of books neatly in the middle of each table alongside a pot of sharpened pencils gives out a loud message to children about the kind of learning that will be taking place. If this is not the preferred learning style of a particular child, then it must be very dispiriting to come into a classroom with that kind of message, day in, day out.

Spaces that are conducive to learning

An increasing amount of research has been carried out into the kinds of environment that are conducive to learning. Traditionally in the UK we have encouraged early years settings that are busy and colourful and full of 'stuff'. However, these kind of environment could be making learning difficult for some children. So, in planning for the space in their classrooms, teachers need to find out more about the impact of three elements in particular:

- noise;
- colour;
- light.

Elizabeth Jarman in her innovative work on 'Communication friendly spaces' (see www.elizabethjarmanltd.co.uk) draws our attention to the impact of these three elements on learning.

Noise

Being in a noisy environment makes it really difficult for children to concentrate. This can not only prevent them thinking about their learning but also has a negative effect on their speaking and listening skills.

Colour

Despite the value of having interesting displays, many are over-stimulating. For many children, bright primary colours may not be conducive to either concentration or learning, and schools need to consider their colour schemes and displays with greater sensitivity to this issue.

Light

We are all energized by natural sunlight and children learn better in spaces with natural light. Light can be used to create mood and define an area – and it is possible to experiment with different levels of light and light sources to see which different children prefer.

Elizabeth Jarman encourages all practitioners to view the learning space from the child's perspective, asking who the environment appeals most to and why, seeing what the space and colours and light look like from a child's-eye view. It is all too easy to create something that appeals to us as adults and, we think, will appeal to other adults who are coming into our rooms. Learning spaces are primarily for children and it is always salutary to talk to them about whether the spaces we have created are conducive for them to learn.

Space for learning out of doors

The EYFS is now unequivocal in its expectation that environments for children up to age 5 should enable both indoor and outdoor learning:

- Being outdoors has a positive impact on children's sense of well-being and helps all aspects of children's development.
- Being outdoors offers opportunities for doing things in different ways and on different scales than when indoors.
- It gives children first-hand contact with weather, seasons and the natural world.
- Outdoor environments offer children freedom to explore, use their senses, and be physically active and exuberant.

(DCSF 2008: Card 3.3)

Nothing changes when these learners become 6! Most Year 1 – and indeed Year 2 children – will choose to learn outdoors if given the chance. If teachers want to optimize children's learning opportunities then it is necessary to offer them the environment of their choosing for much of the time.

> If teachers want to optimise children's learning opportunities then it is necessary to offer them the environment of their choosing for much of the time.

Research into outdoor learning and particularly the 'Forest School approach' shows that, outdoors, children:

- find the real world to explore and investigate;
- experience the natural world in ways that cannot be simulated indoors;

- have opportunities to be 'their natural, exuberant, physical and noisy selves' (White 2008: 2);

- work on a larger scale which often suits their current gross and fine motor development;

- use their bodies in ways that exercises their minds;

- have freedom to be messy and adventurous;

- have opportunities to be quiet and hidden away from adults;

- have endless opportunities to talk, share and discuss – often with more confidence than when indoors;

- have ever-changing opportunities to set themselves challenges and take risks while learning how to keep themselves safe.

Regrettably, many schools are still not designed with an understanding of outdoor learning being much more than 'playtime'. The kind of learning which this book promotes is outdoor learning that:

- takes place when learning is happening indoors also;
- is available from the start of – and throughout – the learning day;
- is as challenging and worthwhile as the learning that takes place indoors (and possibly more so);
- is a teaching and learning environment – and not just one where adults 'supervise';
- is supported and developed by knowledgeable adults.

The kind of learning described above cannot take place in a tarmac rectangle where no thought has been given to the learning opportunities that might occur, and no funding has been given to support the development of that area.

Good outdoor areas for learning have as rich a range of opportunities and experiences as indoors. The outdoors should not be seen as an 'add-on' but is a complete learning environment within itself, providing opportunities to meet the full range of children's needs and not just the physical.

> The outdoors should not be seen as an 'add-on' but as a complete learning environment within itself.

In planning for an outdoor area, therefore, the provision and its organization require every bit as much thought and attention as the indoor environment. A valuable reference for the development of outdoor areas is Early Education's resource pack 'Outdoor Learning in the Early Years' (see www.early-education.org.uk).

In planning an outdoor area staff need to consider the following:

1 The *space* that is available – can it be increased following negotiation with senior staff (see the case studies below)?
2 The way the space is *allocated* – is/are there:

- a hard area;
- a grassy area;
- different levels;
- areas where children can be private;
- areas with shade;
- areas for play that takes up space (e.g. playing with balls and quoits; large circle games; drama and construction) without interrupting other play going on;
- different surfaces underfoot;
- interesting walkways that lead children from one area to another?

This may seem far more than most Key Stage 1 classes can currently provide, but it is so important that we recognize that this is what a 4- or 5-year-old in a good nursery school will experience and ask ourselves why the 5- or 6-year-old in Key Stage 1 shouldn't be entitled to the same. The outdoor area should be on the school's development plan so that everyone is united in working towards quality provision that will benefit all the children in the school.

In her book *Outdoor Play in the Early Years* (2002), Helen Bilton suggests that areas need to be delineated for:

- design, building and construction;
- active and vigorous physical work;

- imaginative play;
- scientific discovery;
- language and mathematical work.

In addition, she adds, 'Space needs to be made available outside for quiet and reflective play, away from others' (2002: 6).

3 The way *resources* are sorted and made available – do children get involved in deciding what should be kept where and are they then responsible for maintaining the organization of the outdoors alongside staff? Is there adequate outdoor storage so that resources can be kept safely when not in use (see below for a broader discussion about resources – both indoors and out)?

Resources that can stimulate children's learning outdoors

- Sandpit (large – think 'golf bunkers' not 'trays').
- Water play – with tubes and guttering, containers and hoses.
- Garden equipment – for digging, planting, watering and so on.
- 'A' frames and trestles (all far more flexible than fixed climbing equipment – and cheaper).
- Wooden planks.
- Metal ladders.
- Milk crates, wooden pallets and other sturdy boxes for building, sitting on and making dens.
- A range of making and designing materials – string, rope, masking tape, scissors etc.
- Large pieces of material – various fabrics in different colours and styles.
- Pieces of carpet and carpet squares.
- Hollow blocks in a whole range of sizes.
- Inserts from carpets, card tubing of different sizes, large cardboard boxes.

- Imaginative play equipment – including puppets, dressing up clothes and accessories.

- Small games equipment – balls, hoops, skipping ropes, beanbags, quoits etc.

- Plastic cones for creating spaces and for games.

- Chairs, benches and cushions for sitting on.

- Drawing and writing materials – everywhere!

- Books in crates.

- Resources for outdoor exploration, such as magnifying glasses.

- Natural materials (see below).

- Spaces for being quiet and having good conversations – tents, gazebos, huts and play houses.

Jan White's highly practical and informative book *Playing and Learning Outdoors* (2008) has one of the best expositions I have read about the values that should underpin high quality outdoor experiences for children. In addition, she emphasizes the 'real-world-ness' of the outdoors, and the benefits for children of exploring and playing with natural materials such as:

- sand and soil;
- wood: logs, tree trunk slices, sections of branches, sticks and twigs;
- stone: cobbles, pebbles, slate, gravel;
- plants: Rowers, petals, herbs, leaves, grass;
- seeds: conkers, acorns, sycamore seeds;
- shells, feathers, minerals.

Her book reminds us of what these natural materials offer children as both the landscape for play and the resources for playing there. The following is a précis of her explanation of the potential of natural resources to support the learning and development of young children.

A good supply of natural materials can do the following

- Respond to the child's insatiable curiosity to explore the stuff of the world around them.

- Provide therapeutic play that is emotionally satisfying and supports mental health. Children often spend long periods of time lost in their own worlds as they handle, manipulate, explore and imagine.

- Promote awareness and emotional connection to the world around: playing with things that belong to the natural world; experiencing seasonal rhythms; enjoying the aesthetic qualities of natural things.

- Encourage the development of sensory systems and sensory integration. Natural materials offer visual, textural, temperature, weight, smell and sound stimuli.

- Develop intellectual skills (e.g. through observing detail, sorting and classifying, the basic skills of recognizing similarities and differences develop).

- Develop both fine manipulative and gross motor physical skills: through, for example, digging or lifting and carrying heavy items such as logs.

- Develop imagination and creativity: their truly open-ended nature means they are very versatile and can be used and combined in endless ways.

- Develop language through playful interaction: for example, using descriptive language for the properties of materials and hearing adults describe what is happening during exploration and play.

(White 2008: 16–17)

Creating space for outdoor learning

As we have already said, not every school has the potential to develop outdoor learning spaces of this quality. But it is still important that we keep our eye on the gold standard so that areas can be developed over time. The first priority is to have as large a space as possible. Sometimes, offering Key Stage 1 children opportunities for free-flow outdoor learning requires some creative decision-making on behalf of senior managers.

Examples of extending space for outdoor learning in Year 1

Case Study 1

A Year 1 class had very little space indoors and the teacher was struggling to provide sufficient opportunities for play. Then the head-teacher sanctioned the creation of a doorway though the Year 1 class-room wall and out onto a small area of concrete. Once the door was in place, a large sandpit was put in and the teacher developed the area alongside her Foundation Stage colleague to maximize learning opportunities outside.

Case Study 2

In a large urban primary school, the Year 1 classes had no possibility of creating an outdoor area for free-flow access. The Year 1 teachers took this problem to their senior management team who decided that they could move the classes around so that the Key Stage 1 children moved into the upper primary classrooms that had doors to the outside that were never used.

Case Study 3

A small village school had no outdoor area for its Key Stage 1 classes. The headteacher was persuaded that an outdoor area for learning was more valuable for Key Stage 1 than a 'playground'. Part of the play-ground was given over to the younger children and developed as a proper outdoor area for learning. At lunchtimes a staggered eating arrangement was put in place so that not all the children needed the playground at the same time.

Resources

Once the space is organized, teachers need to cast a critical eye over the quality of the resources which children will encounter in the classroom and outside.

It was observed in Chapter 5 that many of the best resources are free and can be acquired, after friendly persuasion, from shopkeepers, friends and relatives. Nevertheless, whether resources are free or whether they have had to be purchased from school budgets, there are some rules of thumb to consider if they are to support children's independent learning. Resources in effective environments need to:

- be organized and accessible;
- be maintained by the children;
- reflect the real world;
- be as open-ended as possible.

High quality resources encourage collaboration and conversation

Organized and accessible

To begin with, everything needs sorting and needs to have a 'home'. Experience has shown that the way adults choose to organize and group things does not always work for children – which is one reason why they find it so difficult to keep the spaces tidy. The best strategy seems to be to talk with the children about what needs to be sorted and to get them to decide where things go and how they are grouped and labelled.

Time spent on experiences such as these is never wasted. To begin with there is valuable learning in such activities – problem-solving, negotiation, measuring, data-handling, to name but a few. Then, if children have a vested interest in what goes where, they are more likely to remember the organization and take responsibility for keeping things in their place. It may be that children want to label shelves or apparatus but this might not be necessary for these older children. However, anything that brings about reflective action and prompts the children to write for a purpose can only be a good thing.

One aspect of this organization is that resources must also be accessible. Children need to be able to reach everything without either having to get a friend to move out of the way or interrupting an adult to get something down for them. This means that, as part of the sorting process, thought needs to be given to where resources are stored. Open shelves are best (cupboard doors again take up unnecessary space when they are open, and curtains are just a nuisance). In addition, shelving that is too high just interrupts the learning flow while the child waits for an adult to get what they need.

So, look at the classroom together with the children and decide the following.

- How shall we group resources so that we all know where to find them?
- Have we enough shelving to put everything on display, or do we need to rotate some resources?
- Are shelves currently cluttered with unnecessary 'stuff' that can be stored elsewhere?
- Can all the children reach all the shelves?

Maintained by the children

As well as being fetched and tidied away by the children, resources also need to be maintained by them. For example, if there is a spillage, children know what to do – and have the resources to do it: brooms, dustpans, mops, cloths and so on. Children also need to know what to do if paint runs out, if pencils need sharpening and if glue gets everywhere.

This is such an important element of independent learning that teachers would do well to spend considerable time on it with a new class. It is not possible – and gets very frustrating – if you are trying to get children to be independent while also trying to teach a set of learning objectives to another group of children. Always spend the early days and even weeks of the new school year teaching the children all the skills they need to be independent learners.

> Spend the early days and even weeks of the new school year teaching the children all the skills they need to be independent learners.

This time is well spent, for once they can manage themselves then the teacher has far, far fewer interruptions of a trivial nature to contend with when she should be teaching.

Managing the environment also means managing each other. Children need to learn to negotiate resources, to share space, to help each other tie aprons or whatever it takes to maintain their independence. Rather than put up signs that say, 'Only three children can play here' it can be far more beneficial for children to work out for themselves when space becomes crowded and how then to manage – whether to wait and watch, for example, or whether to leave and move on to something else.

Equally, children of this age need to learn to manage the real-life rough and tumble of sharing the space and resources that are available. Being able to negotiate, being able to wait your turn, being able to use different resources because the thing you wanted is already being used, are all skills that children may have been taught, but which need some practical application in the real world of collaboration and cooperation.

Independent learning for children means managing the space, the resources and each other – and the most effective Key Stage 1 classrooms have children who have been taught to manage all of these.

Reflecting the real world

The world of school is, in itself, a fake world. It has been created artificially and what happens within it is designated almost entirely by adults. Children are drawn to learning in the real world because it makes sense to them and has meaning. Teachers, therefore, have to work hard to make the experiences of children when they are at school as lifelike as possible. Unfortunately, on so many occasions, learning in the classroom seems to be devoid of both sense and meaning to young learners.

Thus teachers should bring real-life resources into the classroom whenever possible. Children are irresistibly drawn to natural resources – cones, leaves, straw and feathers – rather than endless supplies of plastic. This has a number of advantages for schools. To begin with such resources are less expensive than resources from a catalogue. They are also recyclable, so can be easily replaced when they get 'tired'. But more than that, resources – and experiences – need to have meaning for children and those that reflect children's experience and cultures will be all the more irresistible. If there are workmen building an extension to the school, children will want to try on the hard hats, to cordon off areas of the classroom using the workmen's tape and make cups of tea in adult-size mugs. If money is to be spent improving a play area close to the school, children will want to write to the council asking for what they most want to see in that area, draw plans with the help of a mum who is a designer, ask for an interview with the person in charge of play spaces in their LA. The world is full of real-life problems that need solving and, at this age, children love to feel empowered to have ideas and to share them.

Finally, the resources that children have available should mirror the real world that their learning experiences are trying to recreate. Children are naturally drawn to water, to earth and to sand. These materials offer endless learning opportunities, yet the sand and earth and water of real childhoods doesn't come in small rectangular plastic containers. They are found on beaches and in parks and in woods. The sand is expansive enough to cover bays and to make dunes and rock pools; the water flows in streams and in rivers; the earth is deep enough to nurture trees and bushes. So, when planning, designing and budgeting for these resources in Key Stage 1, ensure that all those involved understand that real sand comes from beaches not sand trays; that earth must be deep enough to be dug with spades in order to be explored and excavated; that water should flow and gush and pour with force and momentum. Play in plastic trays can sometimes serve a purpose, but real-world play that draws on children's skills and knowledge, that requires their imagination and creativity, that is exciting and surprising and rewarding, demands vision on the part of the adults if these experiences are to mirror the real world. Nowadays, more than ever, young children miss out on the opportunities enjoyed by generations before – to play in parks and woods and fields – and schools need to work hard to offer play that, in some way, offers these rich learning opportunities that so many have never experienced.

> Schools need to work hard to offer play that, in some way, offers children these rich learning opportunities that so many have never experienced.

Being open-ended

Last of all, resources need to be as open-ended as possible. In primary classrooms it is very usual to find resources that 'have a purpose', that have been bought in order to teach calculation, or phonological awareness, or floating and sinking. Such resources can have value – but they are limited in that they teach what they are designed to teach. The resources that have the greatest potential for learning are those that are sufficiently open-ended to require children's imagination and creativity for them to be used to their full potential; resources that can be something one day and something completely different the next; resources that do not determine the learning that takes place but that can be altered and adapted to support whatever it is that children are wanting to do. For a rich source of ideas and inspiration see the series 'Carrying on in Key Stage 1' from Featherstone Education (www.acblack.com/featherstone).

Stimulating children's independence

The second element of effective environments for independent learning is that they stimulate children's interest sufficiently for them to *want* to learn independently. We saw in Chapter 4 that this does not happen if activities are low-level and if children are just marking time until the adult arrives. High-quality independent activities involve and engage children and keep them involved and engaged until the adult is ready to go to *them* to find out about their learning.

In order for children to want to learn independently, the learning environment must offer resources, experiences and opportunities that are irresistible.

> In order for children to want to learn independently, the learning environment must offer resources, experiences and opportunities that are irresistible.

Children must feel compelled to pick up, to test out, to have a go and to keep trying. This doesn't mean that everything has to over-stimulate children like a whacky television programme or computer game. When teachers know their child development they appreciate that the best environments offer children of this age two distinct kinds of learning, *satisfying* and *provoking*.

Resources and experiences that are 'satisfying'

Play at this age often involves children in returning to loved and familiar themes: – exploring the complex construction of buildings and models, re-enacting scenarios between princes and dragons, being mum in the home corner and phoning for the doctor – all these and many, many more play themes are often played out in children's heads ready for return to school the next day. So children need to know that the play resources necessary to engage in these themes are readily and constantly available. This means that they are satisfying to children at an emotional level ('I need to know they are there'), and at an intellectual level ('I want to revisit these to extend and improve what I have been thinking about and trying out'). Children will most certainly not articulate their feelings in this way, but their repetitive play behaviour is a strong sign that revisiting learning situations is a crucial stage of their development.

Resources and experiences that are 'provoking'

However, if resources are provided only to satisfy children's needs then the environment can become too familiar and, in the end, boring. So the best learning environments also have an element of provocation within them – resources and experiences that make children stop in their tracks and go, h, I didn't expect to see that there'; 'I don't know what that is/does'; 'I haven't seen any of those before'; 'I wonder what I do with those?'; 'That look interesting!'.

However, as with the 'satisfying' elements of the environment, too much provocation is not a good thing. Children who are constantly provoked or stimulated will quickly get worn out! Children, like adults, need to have a day that allows for the ebb and flow of concentration that optimizes learning. Sometimes children need the new and provoking, sometimes they need the familiar and the repetitious. Effective Key Stage 1 environments should have both.

> Sometimes children need the new and provoking, sometimes they need the familiar and the repetitious. Effective Key Stage 1 environments should have both.

Continuous provision

In order to support the 'satisfying' element of children's learning, the classroom needs to be resourced with sufficient equipment that is constantly available – to enable them to return to their well-loved themes and explorations.

Key Stage 1 teachers who had visited the Foundation Stage classes in their schools and who had begun to experiment with a play-based environment in their own classrooms, came up with this wish-list of resources for continuous provision:

- sand play (remember, think 'golf bunkers' not 'trays' if possible);
- water play (again, large and complex rather than small trays);
- earth;
- malleable materials;
- construction;
- role play;
- small-world play (including puppets);
- workshop area for art and design;

- writing materials (everywhere possible);
- books (everywhere appropriate) but including a designated book corner of course;
- large physical play – for climbing, jumping, balancing, throwing;
- quiet spaces for conversations, reflection and reading.

An examination of continuous provision showed the Key Stage 1 teachers in the Oxfordshire Transition Project the following.

1 At this age, children still 'play about with' resources first before playing 'at' something (that's why adult-initiated activities are often based on 'See what you can find out about these materials before I come back').

Children like space for quiet times as well as for active learning

2   Apart from construction materials – which need to be increasingly challenging to meet the improved dexterity of Year 1 children, as well as their greater spatial and technical awareness – continuous provision in Year 1 looks pretty much the same as it does in the Foundation Stage (it is the increased challenge that children bring to using the resources, the increased mastery of play itself and the increase in challenge from the adults that support the play that differentiates it appropriately for older learners; see Fromberg and Bergen 2006).

3   Key Stage 1 children – just like younger children – will often ignore the adult 'purpose' for which some play resources are set up, and use them instead to represent something of their own choosing.

4   Small-world play seems to become more important in Key Stage 1 than role play, possibly because children are better able to manipulate the figures or because they are more comfortable using the characters to represent their imaginative worlds rather than always being the characters themselves.

'Whatever you want it to be'

The teachers in the second year of the Oxfordshire Transition Project were interested in the work of Professor Pat Broadhead (2004) with primary school teachers on the social and cooperative dimensions of play. Broadhead explored how creative and cooperative children became when – rather than having a fixed theme for role play – they had access to open-ended resources in a 'Whatever you want it to be' space.

Following Broadhead's line of thinking, the Oxfordshire teachers found that providing fewer resources often led to greater creativity on the part of their children.

> Providing fewer resources often led to greater creativity on the part of their children.

Large cardboard boxes, enormous pieces of cloth, clothes-horses, swathes of eye-catching material and multicoloured nesting boxes all encouraged the children to create imaginative worlds at the drop of a hat and ensured that these imaginative scenarios did not pass their sell-by date!

> 'It took two goes to get it established. Second time round we placed small boxes, cardboard tubes, large and small notebooks and pens, scarves and ties and a box of small cardboard discs. The play kept changing – first they were going to work (wearing the ties) then it was a shop, then it changed to a café.'
>
> *Nadia: Year 1 teacher*

The role of the teacher in independent learning

This chapter about the learning environment has emphasized the significance of children learning independently – and how effective environments encourage and sustain children's independent learning. However, this can sometimes lead teachers to underestimate the importance of their own role in this environment. It is important to stress that, even when children are learning without an adult alongside them, the role of the adult remains crucial to the quality of that learning.

Firstly, teachers are crucial because they create the environment. It is their insights, their observations of the children, their thoughts and reflections (and often their money) that create environments that support independent learning. So, teachers are extremely important, before the children even arrive in the room.

Secondly, as we have seen, good teachers use the planning and organization of the environment as a real-life learning opportunity for the children. There are a myriad of opportunities for children to plan, to problem-solve, to arrange, to evaluate their own learning spaces – both inside and out. It is the creative and confident teacher that passes such decision-making and consultation on to their class and encourages them to find workable solutions.

Then, as has been said so often, independent learning is not abandoned learning. While many of the children are working independently, the teacher is not idle. She will be either working with an adult-focused activity, or observing or supporting more independent or child-initiated ng. The quality of the organization of the learning environment is ⸻ makes every element of that environment successful.

⸻ teacher is vital in an environment that encourages independent learning – it is just that their role changes (see Chapter 9). The quality of what teachers do is often truly enhanced because the environment supports both quality focused time and high-quality independent enquiry.

Conclusions

Effective learning environments support a range of learning in a range of ways. They reflect the range of learning styles and preferences of the children within them and should in no way inhibit the active and interactive styles that most Key Stage 1 children display. Wherever possible they need to mirror the real world, presenting learning that is purposeful and meaningful for children and not decontextualized from the day-to-day experiences that children encounter away from the school gates. Effective environments are also flexible. They respond to children's current preoccupations and do not hamper or inhibit their investigations – even if these spread all over the floor, or travel from inside to out. They also offer experiences that are both satisfying and provoking in order to meet both the reflective and the dynamic modes of early learning. Finally, to be truly effective, these environments rely on constant evaluation by both children and their teachers in order to optimize every learning opportunity for every child throughout the day.

Things to discuss in your school

- Is space optimized for active and interactive learning – both indoors and out?

- Are resources – both indoors and out – well-organized and easily accessible?

- Do children's experiences offer an appropriate balance between those that are 'satisfying' and those that 'provoke' new learning?

CHAPTER 7

Using observations as evidence of children's learning

Introduction

If teachers want to make practice in Key Stage 1 developmentally appropriate for the children in their classes, then what is planned and provided will be dependent on the observations they have previously made of children's learning.

This book has emphasized that the most robust evidence for attainment and progress at this age is what children *say* and what they *do*. What children write down will never capture the breadth and depth of their current knowledge, because at age 5, 6 and 7, children's writing skills are not sufficiently well-developed. So, teachers have to find a way of giving time to watching and waiting and wondering about children's learning in order to make accurate assessments.

If doing and using observations is new to you, then two previous chapters will support the introduction of observation into your practice. Chapter 2 is a reminder of how children learn at this age and suggests that, if teachers are going to respond to the developmental needs of children in the class, then they have to know about each 'unique child' and not plan for all children to have the same 'Year 1' learning objective. The chapter gives a rationale for why observation of individual children is necessary.

Chapter 4 explains how teachers create time for observation. In order for an individual teacher to have the opportunity to spend time watching and listening to children learning, the rest of the class must be independent. They must be able to get on with high-quality learning that is either adult-initiated or child-initiated, and not interrupt what the teacher is doing. Observation is a valid – indeed crucial – element of adult-focused activity.

It is just that, in this instance, the adult's focus is not directly on teaching a group of children but on observing them.

Observation as a starting point for planning

For many Year 1 teachers, using observation as a starting point for planning will be very different from the methods they currently use. Almost all the teachers in the Oxfordshire Transition Project had been trained to plan using material issued by the Department for Children, Schools and Families and the national strategies. Some were in schools still wedded to the Qualifications and Curriculum Authority (QCA) schemes of work and some had very rigid school schemes of work that curriculum coordinators, in particular, were anxious should be adhered to.

> 'The most terrifying moment for me was when you said "put the files down and look at the children instead". I didn't know what to look for!'
>
> *Pat: Year 1 teacher at Project meeting*

Once you start to think about individual children, of course, schemes of work aren't always helpful – nor are they designed for that purpose. Schemes of work give a broad view of how a curriculum subject develops and the stepping stones of subject knowledge, but they cannot provide the information necessary to personalize those curriculum experiences for individual children. Schemes of work are primarily for medium-term planning – to support decisions about what elements of the curriculum should be covered in a term or half term and, if appropriate, linked together through themes or topics (see Chapter 8). But at the medium-term stage, decisions should not be made about how concepts and skills will be taught. This requires first-hand knowledge of children's current needs and interests and cannot be planned in a vacuum. Only first-hand observation of children in action as learners will tell you how a particular child is most likely to become interested in or be stimulated to learn about the next steps.

Making time for observation

Many Year 1 teachers (in actual fact nearly all of them!) said at first that there was 'no time' for observation of children. There were 'too many things' to fit into the day. My reply has always been that if you invest time in observation you will *save time* planning experiences or activities that are either beyond a child's ability, or do not stretch and challenge him, or simply do not interest him because his own current interests have been ignored.

> If you invest time in observation you will *save time* planning experiences or activities that are either way beyond a child's ability, or do not stretch and challenge him.

Using 'the triangle' (see Figure 4.1) as the basis for classroom planning will enable observation to be a daily part of classroom life. It is important for teachers to be convinced that observation is a legitimate teaching activity. This is a point I make vociferously to headteachers because so many teachers say they feel guilty if the head walks in and they are – apparently – 'doing nothing'. I explain to heads that watching, listening and noting are some of the most valuable – and skilled – things that a teacher can do. It means that you will *know* what a child needs, and not *presume*. It means that you will understand what excites and enthuses them, and not guess. It means you will differentiate appropriately, and not by arbitrary grouping against random criteria.

> 'I can't believe how well I know the children now. My reports are so much better this year because I really know what each individual can do and is interested in.'
>
> *Sue: Year 1 teacher*

'I know the children so well because we have made time to observe them and talk to them properly. Even though it has been a large class this year I feel like I know them better than any class I've had. It worries me that I probably knew these children better in half a term than I ever knew any of my previous classes.'

Pat: Year 1 teacher

'Reports have gone out to parents and I have had lots of feedback about how well I know the children – I am really pleased!'

Sue: Year 1 teacher

'Observation has been crucial – by observing and listening to children we are able to create situations and activities which inspire children and are based on knowledge of their current interests. This has led to a need to plan daily so planning can be derived from both the day's experiences and children's requests and responses.'

Shona: Year 1 teacher

Different kinds of observation for different occasions

Using 'the triangle' (Figure 4.1) we can see that there are different occasions when observation can take place for different purposes.

Adult-focused activity

During adult-focused activity you may engage in what Margaret Edgington (2004) calls 'participant jottings' – i.e. noting significant learning as you sit with an individual or a group. These can be done on a post-it, in a notebook or onto a sticky label that can be stuck straight into a record/profile book.

Equally, you may step back from teaching and, instead, choose to observe an activity where children are learning independently, or observe an individual child or group of children for a particular purpose. This may be because you have concerns about a particular child or because you have noticed there are some gaps in the profile of their learning that you have been accumulating.

Such longer observations can be recorded on a sheet such as that shown in Figure 7.1 and kept as part of the child's profile or as part of your short-term planning (as evidence of why you are planning what you are planning).

Adult-initiated activity

As we saw in Chapter 4, once an adult-focused activity is completed, the teacher returns to activities she has initiated but then left in order for the children to get on independently. When the teacher returns to an adult-initiated activity it is not always necessary or desirable to join in straight away with what the children are doing. Some moments spent observing the activity, and the individual children engaged in it, will tell the teacher the following:

- Whether children have understood the challenge that was posed. (Was it an effective adult-initiated activity? Were the children deeply engaged? Was it sufficiently open-ended? Did the children think the problem posed was worth solving?),

- Whether children have moved on from the original problem and followed their own interests in a different learning direction. (If so, what are the children's interests? What was the thinking behind their change of direction?),

- What the group – or individual children – is/are trying to achieve, what they are exploring and thinking (so that the teacher's first question tunes straight into their *thinking* and doesn't just seek to establish 'what are you *doing*?').

These observations may just stay in the teacher's head to inform her knowledge of the children involved. Or it may be that the teacher notices something significant ('I didn't know whether so-and-so understood that'; 'I thought so-and-so had grasped that!') and, as has been suggested earlier, this can be jotted on a post-it or sticky label and put into a profile or planning book at a later stage.

Figure 7.1 Exemplar observation planning sheet

Exemplar observation/planning sheet

Child: **Date:**

Length of observation:

Context:
Is learning inside/outside? Is it adult-focused; adult-initiated; child-initiated? Is child learning alone/with others?

Observation:
What does the child say/do?

Next steps:
What learning/resources/experiences does the child need next?

Child-initiated activity

The fascination of child-initiated activity is that it is so unpredictable. When an adult goes to observe what children are exploring or developing, then they often have to spend some considerable time finding out what play themes are being pursued on that particular occasion. This makes child-initiated learning very challenging to observe because the adult is looking and listening with no preconceived expectations about what might be being learned. It is all too easy (and most early years teachers have done it at some point) to bowl into a play situation, assume that you know what is going on, ask a daft question and kill the play stone dead.

> It is all too easy to bowl into a play situation, assume that you know what is going on, ask a daft question and kill the play stone dead.

It is easy, for example, to assume that because the children are, say, in the block corner, and that they are building, say, towers, then they are interested in tower building, when in fact they may well be playing out a scenario they have seen on television, creating a story to which the blocks are secondary, or exploring concepts of height or balance rather than being interested in the end product of 'a tower'.

Jumping to the wrong conclusions can be all too easy. So observation of play needs time. It also requires adults who are intrigued and impressed by children's thinking and their powers of imagination and creativity. Watching children play means using every ounce of curriculum and child development knowledge to move the observation from:

- What are they doing? *to*
- What are they learning? *or*
- What are they showing me they know?

> Observation requires adults who are intrigued and impressed by children's thinking and their powers of imagination and creativity.

The message from the Oxfordshire Project teachers is: make time for observation and just have a go! Only by starting to understand play – in order to see its themes emerging, to see what different children do with similar resources, to see the roles children take on in different scenarios – will you start to understand the richness and power of play as a vehicle for learning and realize how limiting so many adult-initiated activities can be. If using observation is new to you, then here are some suggested strategies for getting started.

Starting to use observation

1 Identify one time a day for observation of children's play.

2 Spend at least 20 minutes observing and listening (you may need to build up to this as your class becomes more independent and stops asking, 'What are you doing?').

3 See what patterns of play emerge over several days. Do the same children play together? Do the same children choose the same play activities? Do children return to enacting certain themes? Do the resources seem to challenge and engage the children?

4 Start to use the interests children have in their play to plan for the learning environment and other – perhaps more adult-focused or adult-initiated – learning experiences the following day.

Observing children requires time to be attentive and intrigued

Example of observation leading to planning, from Year 1 teachers' logs

1 'I saw that the children had replaced the measuring jugs in the water tray with boxes from the modelling table. They were interested in the speed with which the water ran through materials (e.g. cardboard), and spent a long time talking to each other and devising different effects. The next day I asked if they would like to thicken the water with "jellibath" and put jugs and junk-modelling materials there for them to continue their experiments.'

2 'A group of children were playing in the sand tray. There was a selection of kitchen-type stuff in there – pans, spoons, jugs. I observed they were making cakes and were using some vocabulary correctly – mix, pour, stir, etc. To further this and enhance the vocabulary I planned next day for some "real" cake making. Children worked nearly independently to produce cup cakes. All

ingredients were weighed to match the weight of an egg (it's based on an old German recipe aka pound cake).'

3 'A group of girls started going round the class with clipboards asking people if they wanted to go to their party and writing the names down on a list. Then they decided to make a cake from Playdough and give that to someone. This continued for a couple of days so I added candles, patti tins, invitations, party hats etc. to the Playdough to enhance the learning and respond to their interests.'

4 'A group of more able girls were joining construction materials in a long line along the floor. This went on for most of the morning and different children came and went. There was a lot of discussion about how far around the room, the art area and even the corridor they could get it to reach. They then began counting all the separate pieces to see how many they had used. They lost interest at this point and left. The next day some of the children involved resurrected the activity and the TA suggested getting metre sticks and tape measures and clipboards to measure and record how far the "line" went.'

Two key purposes of observation

Observation has two key purposes. The first is to find out as much as possible about the child as a learner. The second is to use that information to provide the appropriate next steps of children's learning.

Finding out about the child

Building a rounded profile
Observation helps teachers to tune in to what an individual child is trying to achieve; what they are interested in; who they like to be with; the roles they take on; whether they are struggling or being challenged. Each moment spent in observation will add another piece of the jigsaw that makes up the 'unique child' and their particular strengths and needs.

It is important, therefore, to get as many angles on the child as possible; to see the child from a number of perspectives. In this way you will achieve a rounded view of the child as a learner and not one that only tells you what the child is like when they answer questions on the carpet, or when they are a learner in an activity led by an adult. Very often children show us quite different sides of themselves when they are engaged in different kinds of learning situations, and if we only observe one kind of learning then our view of the learner will be impoverished.

> If we only observe one kind of learning then our view of the learner will be impoverished.

If we are to build this more rounded view of each individual child then that means taking into account a number of things.

1   Observe the child at different times of the day – we are all larks or owls; not all children learn best in the mornings.

2   Observe during different kinds of session – is the child different as a learner when an adult is there as opposed to when they are learning with their peers or alone?

3   Observe through different 'lenses' – in other words get observations from a range of people. We all have biases and prejudices and they come out when we do an observation, so see what someone else sees and then compare observations.

4   Make sure you include parents' and carers' views of the child. Parents and carers have insights into a child's learning, their interests, their anxieties, their achievements that you may never know about unless you ask.

5   Make sure the child's own voice is heard in these observations. What does the child believe to be their strengths? What do they enjoy learning about and how do they think they learn best?

Case study

In one primary school, all children have a learning profile. This book is full of photos and annotated comments by the teacher, the parents and the child. The profile goes home every week (or more frequently if the child wants it to) so that the family, including the child, can add photos or comments about things that have happened out of school.

Outings, family celebrations, badges gained and tournaments partici-
pated in are all recorded and returned to school so that the teacher
knows about these aspects of the child's life that she would normally
miss and which, in turn, helps her tune in to the child's needs and
interests as a learner at school.

Consulting the children

In one school, the Year 1 teacher asked her class what helped them
with their learning. The children told her:

- playing and finding things out;
- friends and people we are working with;
- a grown-up;
- things around us in the classroom.

This shows a high level of independence in the children's thinking
and learning. These children understand that there are a range of
ways of learning and that they can draw on a range of resources –
including the teacher – in order to find out more. They have also
understood that play is about learning and that *through* play they
become more effective learners.

Tuning in

So far we have considered observation for the purpose of 'building a
rounded view' of the child as a learner. But there is another facet to observation which is about 'tuning-in to' the child's current thinking.

If planning is to meet the needs of individual learners then we need
observations to ensure that we are building on what children actually do
know and are interested in, rather than making assumptions that 'this is
what they need'.

Tuning-in to children often means the teacher, apparently, 'doing nothing' (the body, rather than the mind). While conversations can reveal a
great deal, there are times when being silent is the best policy (more of this
in Chapter 9).

By the time children reach Year 1 they have learned what is expected of
them as a 'pupil'. They have learned the rituals of lining up, putting your hand

up, waiting your turn and sitting and listening and, while they may not be skilled at all of these, they know there is a certain way of behaving in a school and a classroom. Regrettably, this can seriously inhibit many children. They become more concerned with the rituals, about the rights and the wrongs, about pleasing the teacher, than they are with the business of learning.

Observation of the Oxfordshire Project's DVD material showed that children are often more free to think what they want to think, try out and test out what they want to investigate, put forward an opinion or idea when the adult is *not* there. Somehow, the presence of an adult suggests to children that there is 'one way' of doing something, that there is one answer (the one 'in the teacher's head') and, in either case, their task as pupils is to find out what the *teacher wants* from *them*. So, a view of the child that only ever comes from observing what they do when in a group with an adult, will be a very skewed view indeed.

> A view of the child that only ever comes from observing what they do when in a group with an adult will be a very skewed view indeed.

Tuning-in to children means observing how they go about things and also listening to what they say. It means genuinely being interested in the threads of their thinking so that, as the teacher, we can then build on, supplement and extend these in interesting and varied ways.

Tuning-in requires patience and appreciation. There is a wonderful quote from the preschool educators in Reggio Emilia, Italy, that says 'Listening is a time of long pauses'. That, very gently, means that adults mustn't feel the need to fill the silence. They mustn't fill the silence with unnecessary questions or comments. They mustn't feel that something has to be said for learning to continue. My experience is that adult comments very often inhibit children's thinking if the adult hasn't tuned in successfully to what is preoccupying a group at that time.

Next steps in learning

It is no use gathering lots of observations without doing anything with them. If finding time for observation is difficult then it has no justification if the evidence teachers gather is not promptly used to modify what has been *planned* to meet what has been *discovered* about children's learning needs. Observations of children will help teachers plan the next steps in children's learning, but only if the teacher's short-term plans are sufficiently flexible to accommodate new-found knowledge about the child in this way (see Chapter 8).

In the Oxfordshire Project, we used DVD material to share sequences of children at play and then discussed what the next steps of learning might be. There are many commercially produced sequences of play on the market (although many are not sufficiently long and have music and commentary that might need to be turned down), but it is really valuable to share thinking about this tricky aspect of the assessment and planning process.

In order to support the use of their observations to inform their planning, the Oxfordshire teachers devised the following prompts.

Using observations to provide the next steps in children's learning

1 Only record observations that are 'significant' – that give you new insights into the child as a learner.

2 Use the observations regularly – or they will become out of date, and so will your planning.

3 Discuss the observations, whenever you can, with another adult who knows the child. Your nursery nurse or TA is best – or the Foundation Stage teacher who may have more experience of using observations in this way.

4 Do not assume that what the child is *doing* is what they are *learning.* Sometimes children engage in 'doing' in a rather distracted way and their conversations reveal they are preoccupied by something quite different.

5 Do not assume that if children are involved in something today that you have to give them 'more of the same' tomorrow. Sometimes children are building – but the more important learning is taking place in the story that is being created as they build. 'More block play' will not necessarily be the right thing tomorrow.

---

6 Look for emerging themes in children's play. Ensure that resources are not 'tidied away' if a play theme is still going strong.

7 Become skilled at what resources to 'add to' a play scenario so they prompt fresh thinking but do not interfere with children's preoccupations.

Using assessment to inform planning

Observations will help teachers plan not only for the needs of individual children, but also for the whole class and for the classroom environment.

Planning the learning environment: continuous provision

Observation of children or a particular activity can tell you whether you have the right balance between 'satisfying' and 'provoking' resources and experiences (see Chapter 6).

Observation of play scenarios will tell you whether you have located resources in accessible and appropriate places – is everything used? If not, why not?

Planning for individual children: differentiated provision

Observation of individual children will enable you to introduce and adapt learning to suit a child's particular needs and interests. However, meeting the needs of individual children does not mean that every child will need something different every day. Often, children are at similar stages of development and there will be overlap in terms of the concepts and skills that are to be introduced. On the other hand, it is fascinating how one child's interests can be taken up by a larger group of children and so individual interests become group interests.

Planning for groups of children: enhanced provision

A great deal of play in Year 1 is group-based. Children are generally more sociable and cooperative in their play than in the Foundation Stage, so often children are exploring similar themes and ideas together. An alert adult, who is responsive to these developing ideas, will become skilled at adding fresh resources or a new challenge that keeps the momentum of the play going without interfering with or derailing it (more on this skill in Chapter 9).

Examples from teachers' logs of adding resources to a play scenario

1 'The clay was out with no tools so that children could use their hands to experience its qualities. They were very imaginative in their use of it and after a few days a theme emerged for some of them of making an impression with hands, thumbs, fingers and looking at detail. A box of additional natural materials was put near by and a whole array of impressions started to be created and I was able to link this to the fossils seen recently in the Natural History Museum.'

2 'A group of children were digging outside in the sandpit and found a small piece of silver paper. This became "treasure" and the children proudly showed me their "hoard" when I went to observe. I went and got an ornate wooden box from inside for them to use as a treasure chest. This extended the play so they became pirates, roaming the seas and drawing treasure maps.'

3 'The other week some water had been left overnight in the water tray and had frozen into a really thick, strong layer. The children were fascinated (especially as one or two implements had frozen into it). A group of them tried all means to pull the objects out, and various tools including spades and spoons to crack into the ice. Practitioners watched and listened to the discussion – the children suggested water to melt the ice and hot and cold was fetched – even warm water made very little impression. It remained cold all day and the children devised various means to "attack" the ice, discovering all sorts of properties of it by scraping and hitting it. Practitioners added magnifying glasses and small pots so that the children could explore ice in smaller quantities. As it was another cold night it was decided to put out other containers of different sizes, and some pieces of different sorts of material to freeze overnight nearby. Again the children were fascinated and spent a long time – more questions were raised when it was agreed that other things than water could freeze. As it seemed to be of such interest to many children, different forms of ice were created and explored inside as well.'

Evidence of learning

As has already been emphasized, observations and assessments contribute significantly to evidence of children's learning and development. While most teachers understand and appreciate this, many report ongoing battles with members of senior management teams who ignore such evidence in favour of 'books' or 'pieces of writing'. It is so important that everyone responsible for gathering and analysing evidence of children's attainment and progress understands the quality of the evidence they are asking for.

As previously pointed out, the problem with 'books' and 'pieces of writing' at this age is that children's thinking is way in advance of their writing skills. So, if they are asked to write about, say, their scientific understanding, then what they write may be a very simplified version of what they know and understand. At age 6 and 7, for most children, the only useful evidence that writing can provide is of writing development.

> At age 6 and 7 the only useful evidence that writing can provide is of writing development.

Writing doesn't necessarily show mathematical understanding, scientific knowledge, or even imagination and creativity. All of these are still much richer and more accurate in oral or pictorial form than they are in written form – especially when children are still at an age when they are mastering the manipulation of a pencil. So, until the time when children's writing is a true reflection of their understanding and ability, the best 'evidence' base comes from observations *by* adults *of* children's learning.

This leaves teachers of younger primary age children with a problem. How do senior teachers – many of whom have only had teaching experience of older primary age groups – come to understand that what they are asking for may not only be unavailable (best practice in Key Stage 1 does not ask for considerable amounts of written work) but may also be unreliable. The fact of the matter is that the only way for all teachers to learn about evidence of children's learning is for them to understand more about children's learning at different ages.

Conclusions

Without making time for observation, it is not possible to provide a learner-centred curriculum. The turning point for many teachers comes when they realize how much better they know their children through these observations and how much more satisfying that makes their teaching. When observations become a daily part of a teaching routine, then teachers find their planning is far more appropriate and the activities they prepare far more meaningful for the children. This can only mean that both adults and children enjoy a more rewarding learning day. There is no doubt that the more that teachers get to know children the more they give time to observation – convinced that it is the way to engage and motivate individual learners.

CHAPTER 8

Planning for adult-initiated and child-initiated learning

Introduction

When teachers think about changing their practice, they often ask for planning formats to support the changes they want to make. I always refuse! My firm belief is that planning comes at the very end of the process of reflection, change and evaluation of practice. Once a classroom is set up for independent learning alongside adult-led learning; once play is a key component of the child's learning day; once observation of both adult-initiated and child-initiated learning is part of the teacher's daily routine – *then* planning takes care of itself. Unless a teacher is going to ignore the evidence of her own eyes, then the information gleaned from observations of learning will lead naturally into ways of planning that support a developmentally appropriate curriculum.

This, of course, is in complete contrast to the orthodoxy beloved of those who do not subscribe to learner-centred practice and want to control all that children do and what they learn in the course of a day; where planning has come to dictate practice rather than the other way round. But all teachers need to question the purpose of planning, for it does not have a life in its own right. Its only purpose is to ensure that teachers think about and are prepared for what each of their children need in order to have a challenging and rewarding learning experience day in, day out. As such, planning should be the servant of practice and not its mistress.

> Planning should be the servant of practice and not its mistress.

It is imperative that this is understood by senior managers. Schools where teachers are required to complete a school planning format have managers who do not understand the differing demands of planning for learning at different stages within the primary age range. What is a relevant and appropriate planning process for a class of children in Year 4 or 6 may be quite inappropriate for Years 1 and 2. Good headteachers understand that all that is required of planning is that it produces good learning outcomes, not that it has a consistent format from one year group to the next.

Perhaps the greatest myth to have taken hold over recent years is that what is planned is what is learned. This is a false premise on which to operate. However carefully and thoughtfully teachers plan for learning, learners often have other ideas, especially at this age when, as we have seen, children are still driven by their own preoccupations and interests and it is foolhardy to imagine that the teacher's transmission of knowledge, skills or understandings will be dutifully picked up and learned by all children.

The impact children make on planning

When planning, we must dispel the notion that because a child is in Year 1 they will learn what all other Year 1 children should learn. Although a class of children is usually made up of pupils who are born within one calendar year, their actual development may span two or more years, and teachers know that they must pay close attention to and plan for the differences between their children rather than trying to treat them as a homogenous whole.

Some children who are in Year 1 will still need to be working within the Foundation Stage curriculum while others are ready to address far more complex skills and understandings. And, of course, children are not necessarily 'able' or 'less able' across the whole curriculum. Some children may be advanced in their literacy skills, for example, but need greater help and support in maths or social development.

Learning at this age is neither sequential nor is it predictable. Just because one aspect of the curriculum is covered on Monday does not mean that all children will be ready for the same 'next step' on Tuesday. This is true even among a small group of children let alone if a teacher tries to teach an aspect of the curriculum to the whole class. Children lurch from one learning stage to another according to many factors. They can race ahead and then plateau for a while, then seemingly lose ground – all at different times and for different reasons. Any teacher who attempts to teach all children the same objective at the same time in the same way, marching relentlessly from one learning objective to the next, is only covering the curriculum – not teaching children.

As a starting point for planning it is crucial to establish what children's previous learning experiences have been. Children do not arrive in the classroom as empty vessels. What a child learns in the course of the day depends on a complex matrix of past experiences and current concerns.

> What a child learns in the course of the day depends on a complex matrix of past experiences and current concerns.

Too many teachers plan as though what a child will learn or needs to learn is dependent on the previous learning experiences they have had *in school*. But this is to ignore the profound impact of children's learning away from the school environment. Children come from homes, from families, from communities that are rich in experiences that touch on every aspect of school learning. School learning is the icing on the cake. When it is of good quality it can make learning more systematic, but schools should never be so presumptuous as to act as though they are the only conveyors of knowledge. When teachers plan to introduce something new they should always ask, 'What do *these* children in *this* class already know?' (for it will change from year to year); 'What might some of the children be able to teach each other – and me – about this aspect of their experience?'

Finally, what a child will learn will be affected by the mood they are in and their preoccupations at the time. We have already seen that young children have an immense internal drive to pursue learning that they are interested in, to follow up things that they have instigated. Unless what the teacher has initiated is seen as worthwhile and unless the child is secure in knowing that there will be a time in the day when their own interests can be pursued, the teacher may lose the battle for the mind of the child (even if the child's body language suggests they are paying attention).

Then again, the child may not be learning effectively because their mind is outside the classroom completely. As was seen in Chapter 3 a child who has had no breakfast, a child who has left the house with the abusive words of a parent ringing in their ears, a child who knows they have to go home to care for a sick relative, will not necessarily be able to focus their attention on the teacher's intentions and may find it hard to concentrate and to be tuned in to the teacher at all.

Stages of planning

When teachers are concerned about meeting children's developmental needs, then the stage of planning that is affected most is *short-term planning*. While most schools require planning at three stages – long, medium and short term – it is mainly at the short-term stage that teachers need to make the adjustments to their plans that take account of what observations have shown them about children's learning needs.

In order to explain this to others, I have found it helpful to differentiate between the purposes of planning at these three stages. For me, long- and medium-term planning are about the *curriculum* and short-term planning is about the *child*.

> Long- and medium-term planning are about the *curriculum* and short-term planning is about the *child*.

At the *long-term* stage the teacher ensures that all statutory requirements of the curriculum are met and that any additional aspects of the curriculum that are particular to the school or the children are identified and recorded.

At the *medium-term* stage the teacher decides how that curriculum can be divided up: which bits of the curriculum go with which other bits and whether there are themes or topics that might bring about a more meaningful curriculum experience for the children.

The planning and organization of the curriculum at the long and medium stages are applicable to most children at a given age and in a given year group. Although we have already seen that being 5, 6 or 7 does not bring with it an automatic set of needs and abilities, the National Curriculum does lay down a set of skills and concepts that should be taught to children at these ages. It is salutary to remember however, that the National Curriculum – the only statutory curriculum for Key Stage 1 children – does not differentiate between Years 1 and 2, but rather leaves the design of the curriculum to the professional judgement of teachers.

Schools are increasingly returning to this more creative way of managing curriculum planning. The final report of The 'Independent Review of the Primary Curriculum (DCSF 2009) emphasizes the necessity for cross-curricular learning bearing in mind 'the distinct but interlocking ways in which children learn and develop' (para. 7). It reminds schools that cross-curricular learning 'strengthens subjects' and encourages children to 'apply what they have learned' (para. 25). Most hopeful of all is that the report states that the new Primary Curriculum: 'Gives schools much more flexibility to plan a curriculum that meets national entitlement and much more discretion to select curriculum content according to their local circumstances and resources' (DCSF 2009: para. 2.16).

It is so important that schools seize this opportunity and begin to look creatively once more at how the curriculum is designed for children.

The short-term stage

Although the long and medium stages of planning are significant, they are not about individual children. They are not about Joe, or Nadeem or Sally or Moses. They are not about the child with special needs, the child with English as an additional language, the child living in a refuge, the child whose grandma has just died. They are not personal and not – yet – relevant, to the individual learner.

Planning for individual children takes place at the short-term stage, once a class is met, once personalities are established, once idiosyncrasies are known. It is at this stage that we stop presuming what children might need and want, and come to *know*. At the short-term stage teachers use their observations and assessments of the children in their class – who may be the same age but may be utterly different in their needs from the Year 1 or Year 2 class they had last year.

Asking for planning in advance

The flexibility required of high quality short-term planning has ramifications for those who ask for teachers' planning in advance. Any teacher who is planning to meet the learning needs of children using their daily observations cannot know on Monday what a child might be learning on Friday.

> Any teacher who is planning to meet the learning needs of children using their daily observations cannot know on Monday what a child might be learning on Friday.

When confronted by heads who make such demands I ask them what they want the planning for. If it is to see what the teacher intends to cover, then planning can indeed be handed in at the beginning of the week. If, however, it is to establish what children have actually learned, then, as we have seen, this is unpredictable and can only be reported retrospectively. If a headteacher wants planning in on a Monday, then I suggest they receive planning for Monday and possibly Tuesday of the week to come and then *retrospective* planning for the previous Wednesday, Thursday and Friday. In this way the teacher is not 'making up' what might happen on the latter days of the week, but can give an accurate report of what was covered and what was learned the previous week.

Schemes of work

Schemes of work can make a valuable contribution to our knowledge of curriculum development. While early years and primary teachers remain generalists there will always be aspects of the curriculum with which they are more confident than others. The problem with schemes of work is when they overstep the mark for which they were intended. While it is fine for schemes of work to show the path of progression in skills and concepts for different areas of the curriculum, they become problematic when they start to prescribe the activities or topics that should be 'taught' as a result.

> 'I can't bear our school schemes of work. Sometimes the topics they expect my little 5-year-olds to be interested in are farcical. Whoever designed them has never taught Year 1!'
>
> *Shona: Year 1 teacher*

'I think at present our Year 1 curriculum becomes compartmentalized too quickly. We are trying to look at this in the light of the recommendations in *Excellence and Enjoyment* and the ideas about the creative curriculum. We no longer follow the Literacy and Numeracy Hours but elements of these over the week. This helps offer children a more integrated set of learning experiences.'

Sara: Year 1 teacher

While we can think about what elements of the curriculum we might want to introduce to children in the abstract, we cannot know the vehicle for doing so effectively until we know the children. So the same set of skills and concepts may be introduced to one class through a theme of dinosaurs, while for another it may be birthdays or journeys. It may be that not all of the class will be interested in the same theme. One group may have seen a film together as a birthday treat and be 'into' pirates, while another may be fascinated by materials and making something together. The creative skill of the teacher is in knowing what themes will be relevant and meaningful to her class at any particular time.

Of course it is much easier to follow a topic cycle so that if it's spring term of Year 1 it must be 'Transport'. But what if your class aren't interested in transport at the moment? I have seen so many children struggle to find any fascination with a teacher-planned theme – such as 'Florence Nightingale' – when they might have learned about 'Famous People' far more successfully through studying *The X Factor, High School Musical* or the World Cup.

One good development over recent months has been a relaxing of the expectation that subjects of the Primary Curriculum be taught as discrete elements. The government's own *Excellence and Enjoyment* (DfES 2003) heralded a more flexible approach to curriculum planning and many schools are now embracing with enthusiasm and relief a more cross-curricular approach where elements of subjects that naturally and sympathetically relate to each other are taught together so that children learn to apply their knowledge across subject boundaries. As we have already seen,

The Independent Review of the Primary Curriculum (DCSF 2009), while emphasizing that different approaches to teaching the curriculum all have their strengths, states unequivocally that primary children should have: 'opportunities . . . to benefit from rich, cross-curricular studies which make connections between subjects and encourage pupils to apply what they have learned in one subject to others, thus reinforcing learning and deepening their understanding' (DCSF 2009: p.33, para. 2.9).

Many teachers will be relieved that the curriculum is being reviewed in order to be freed of the constraints that someone else has designed and which have frequently got in the way of responding to the needs of children within their own classes.

'Interestingly the QCA scheme of work for Year 1 is to teach that plants need sun, water etc. to grow. The Year 1 and Reception (mostly) already knew this so it has shown the need to extend this, otherwise I would have just taught it regardless, not knowing they already knew it. We had some fabulous questions about growing.

- How do you grow potatoes, strawberries, cabbages etc.?
- How do marshmallows grow?
- Do stones grow?

This started quite a debate. Sam said that stones don't grow.

Me: Do you actually know that or do you just think it?

Sam: I think it.

Me: Why do you think that?

Sam: Because stones are hard.

Jack: Bones are hard and they grow!

Had I just stuck to the schemes of work I would never have discovered what the children know and the connections they are making.'

Pat: Year 1 teacher's log

Good planning responds to what children show us they already know and can do and allows teachers to find creative solutions to match the curriculum to the children and not the other way around.

> Good planning allows teachers to find creative solutions to match the curriculum to the children and not the other way around.

Timetables

The element of planning that had most impact on the Oxfordshire Transition Project teachers was reviewing their timetables and the impact these were having on how children were learning. In a nutshell, it became obvious that most school timetables interrupt children's learning.

> Most school timetables interrupt children's learning.

If you study a Key Stage 1 timetable, it can be seen that frequently in the course of a day children are required to stop, tidy up, pack away, line up, go to, come back from, unpack, start again. Every time this happens, precious learning opportunities are lost.

This is of particular significance for children in Key Stage 1 because they still need long periods of uninterrupted time for learning – especially when the learning is self-initiated. At age 5 to 7, children are still novice learners. They are still getting to grips with an unending avalanche of new skills and understandings – and this takes time. At this age, children have few secure skills and competencies compared with an adult. Each time a young child comes upon something new it takes longer to work out how it fits with what is already known and understood. So young children need to be given the time for this to happen successfully. This is not possible if, just at the moment when the child might have grasped what they have been grappling with, they are told to 'pack up', 'line up', or 'tidy up'.

The more the Oxfordshire Project teachers looked at their timetables, the more they could see that an inordinate amount of time was spent *interrupting* learning. There were assemblies, playtimes, TV slots, PE lessons, ICT suite times, all of which demand that children stop what they are doing – go somewhere else – and then come back and pick up where they left off or change tack completely and start another subject.*

It became obvious that, if young children need long periods of sustained learning, then the chopped-up nature of their current learning day had to addressed. Over the course of many weeks, the Oxfordshire teachers set about negotiating the timetable with their headteachers, and discussing the place of some traditional features of the school day, as discussed in the following sections.

Registration

It is a legal requirement for schools to know which children are on site at the beginning of the day. But sitting everyone down on the carpet is not necessarily the best way of doing this. Some children come to school dying to tell their best friend some news and find it almost impossible to sit still and be quiet at the start of the day. Some children arrive at school without breakfast or after a family row (which may be a regular feature of their lives), and their heads are simply not in a place to listen and take note. Some children have been cooped up in a small flat or kept indoors because of the weather and are itching to run around, to jump and shout and be physically active and let off steam before they are ready to settle.

None of these children benefits from a start to the day that is controlled and controlling. They will benefit (and the rest of the day will benefit) from a start that allows some chat, some catching up (we all do it when we see our friends at aerobics class or at a match or in the staffroom) and some freedom of movement. Many children who know they are free to do something active as soon as they arrive will plan this at home. They will think about finishing a model or writing an invitation or completing a book or trying to jump off the higher bar of the climbing frame. When you are looking forward to something it is hard to concentrate on something else that is on the adult's agenda.

All of us take a while to settle to serious learning (as I write this book I know I will take up to an hour doing fiddly, less important jobs as I free my mind of the rest of my life and can really concentrate on the words on the page). Yet schools are notorious for expecting the unreasonable of children.

---

* It is important at this stage to say that the teachers were not challenging these features per se, but rather asking the question, 'Given that time is finite, are these aspects of the school day *more* important than children spending time on more sustained learning?'

It is as though we think that it is a sign of our control of children that we can get them to sit from the moment they come in. Maybe we think it impresses the parents that there is order and ritual when they come into the classroom. Whatever the reason, it is a strain for all but the best behaved of our (usually) girls to sustain, and often means we start the day with grumbles and reprimands.

It can be far better to let children come into class and self-register. By Year 1 all children are capable of making either marks on a whiteboard or even signing the register itself to let the teacher know who is present and who is not. It is a great way to get children to practise writing their name for a purpose and gives them a sense of responsibility. Children are then free to undertake some relatively relaxed activities so they can catch up with their friends and the teacher can catch up with parents and the 101 things there are to do at the start of the day. Then, when everyone has got the chatter out of their system, the day can begin with a whole-class session to enthuse and inspire the children about the day ahead and to do any brief whole-class activities that have been planned.

Whole-class teaching

One of the aspects of practice with which the Oxfordshire teachers were universally unhappy was whole-class teaching. For most of them these whole-class sessions didn't meet the needs of the vast range of children they had in their class. While the teachers agreed there was some place for whole-class teaching (see Chapter 4), it was too dominant as a teaching strategy and they wanted to reduce the time spent in this way.

We know that whole-class teaching often brings about a certain kind of learning. It involves what Guy Claxton (1997) refers to as 'slick answers to quick questions' where the mind is required to think on its feet and to think fast. While such learning is valuable in certain situations it certainly is not valuable for most of the more profound thinking and learning undertaken by the human race. We all know that those people who make major discoveries, those who create great symphonies, those who have great ideas for a novel or a poem, do so when their mind is at its most relaxed and – often – when they are not consciously thinking about anything at all.

That is why many of us have our most creative ideas in the bath, walking along a beach, taking the dog out or lying awake in the small hours of the morning. The most creative thinking does not respond to time schedules and competition to be first with your hand in the air.

> The most creative thinking does not respond to time schedules and competition to be first with your hand in the air.

So, if we want children to really think things through; if we want them to develop their ideas and refine them; if we want them to be original and innovative thinkers, we must give them learning opportunities way beyond those demanding slick answers to quick questions. As we have seen, younger children thrive in smaller groups. They are often less intimidated, they are more willing to get something wrong or to be tentative, they are more likely to have more of a say, than in a whole-class situation.

For all these reasons, the Year 1 teachers in the Oxfordshire Project dramatically reduced the number of whole-class sessions and only used them where they thought it advantageous to the children rather than convenient to them as teachers. This instantly created more learning time.

Assemblies

Collective worship is an important part of every school day, and particularly for those in faith schools. Nevertheless it often comes for the whole school at a time of optimum learning for children: either at the beginning of the morning when children have already had to sit for registration; or in the middle of the morning when children may just have got to a critical point in their understanding only to be stopped and 'tidied up'.

Having collective worship in the classroom sometimes means that teachers can choose a time that does not interfere with other learning. It can come at a time of day that suits a more reflective mood and can be made very personal and relevant according to the issues arising in that class at that time.

Many teachers have now negotiated that they attend one whole-school assembly per week and the rest are held more flexibly within the year group or class.

Playtimes

We have already seen that Year 1 and Year 2 children benefit from an outdoor area of learning every bit as accessible and rich in potential as the ones now expected in the Foundation Stage. Many schools are beginning to rethink their outdoor learning opportunities and are moving classes round to enable younger children to have the classrooms with access to the outdoors. Although some schools simply do not have the space for sufficient outdoor learning, many do, and it requires some strategic thinking on the part of heads and senior staff to work out how to give Key Stage 1 access to this powerful learning resource.

If you are fortunate enough to have access to a good quality outdoor area then children will have all the physical activity they need available all day and, therefore, will not need to go out for a 'playtime'. Having an open door policy to the outdoors (as described in Chapter 5) means that children get the physical, mental and emotional ebb and flow of activity and energy that they need to optimize their learning time.

In some schools there are concerns about losing teachers from the playtime rota. However, with one class fewer out in the playground it does make it easier for the remaining staff and it is my firm belief that we should put the needs of children before the needs of staff.

Another argument is that Year 1 and 2 staff do not get a coffee break. While it is good to have a chance to catch up with other colleagues for a conversation/chat, nursery staff have always taken their comfort breaks – and their tea/coffee breaks – while in the throes of their working morning or afternoon. If children are independently learning it is quite possible to go to the toilet (as long as there is another adult in the room), or to safely sip a refreshing drink while the children are working or playing. It's a great time to do more observations.

Another argument is that, without a playtime, children do not mix with other age groups. However, there are lots of opportunities for this to happen at lunchtimes.

Once again the argument that wins is: look at how much time is wasted by 'going out to play'. Ask for a trial period. See how much more settled your children are. See how much deeper into their play and work they get before being interrupted for lunchtime. See how much more time you have for observation, tuning in and teaching. Armed with this evidence it makes it easier to argue for – or against – any of the issues raised above.

PE

If children have regular access to a well-planned outdoor area for learning this will include opportunities for a great range of physical activity and development. Gymnastic skills of climbing, jumping, balancing, roiling

Child-initiated learning should stimulate and challenge children

and motor skills such as throwing, spinning, bouncing, catching and aiming are all possible – and often far more fun – out of doors. Children will get opportunities for physical development as a daily part of their lives without being constrained by access to hall timetables. My feeling – backed up by discussions with Oxfordshire Year 1 teachers – is that you need an indoor space for dance (although there is nothing lovelier than movement in bare feet with the grass between your toes). There are times when, for a larger group of children, the indoor space to move without distraction to a piece of music or other stimuli makes a hall the best place to be. Otherwise, being locked in only to a hall timetable should not be necessary.

ICT

ICT suites have not always proved effective for teaching younger children as, like whole-class teaching, they require interruption of the learning day. In addition, ICT suites teach children not to see ICT as an integral part of their curriculum experiences and, for that reason, many schools (with the encouragement of their LAs) are returning the computers to the class-room. If teachers want to maintain children's learning momentum, children need the ICT there and then, in the classroom – in good working order.

Snack time

Debates about snack time have raged in early years settings for a number of years. There are very strong arguments for children stopping for sociable time together: time to chat to each other and to an adult; time to be reminded about good manners when eating; time to talk more about and learn about different foods and healthy attitudes to eating. However, snack time can also be a time for interrupting the flow of learning. This book is about meeting children's learning needs when they are 5, 6 and 7 years of age and so, even with snack time, we have to consider that the flow of learning is interrupted and that children's interests and preoccupations may be lost unnecessarily at a crucial time. If we are serious about giving children sustained periods of uninterrupted learning then it is better to offer a snack as a 'movable feast' where children can break from their activity at a time of their own choosing – when their own learning momentum is ebbing – and be refuelled ready for another burst.

Planning to match 'the triangle' of classroom experiences

Having created as much sustained learning time as possible in the timetable, the next stage of planning is to decide on the balance between adult-focused, adult-initiated and child-initiated learning (see Chapter 4).

It is impossible to give a hard and fast rule about this. The balance will differ from day to day, according to whether you have a full-time TA or you are teaching alone; whether you are experienced and confident in play as a vehicle for learning; and also depends on a number of other variables.

If you are just moving towards this way of working, here are a series of steps that you might consider to begin with.

Step 1

Start by making all the class as independent as possible. In other words, don't begin by controlling everyone and everything and then giving out little morsels of time for play. 'Golden Time' rarely works well (other than the fact that children enjoy relaxation from teacher-directed activity) and 'choosing' still smacks of a reward for when the teacher's work is finished. Deep-level learning and high quality play rarely arise when they are only given a bit of the week or bits of the day. Start by planning a learning environment that is as play-based as the children have experienced in the Foundation Stage (as long as you are emulating good quality Foundation Stage provision). Children will be familiar with what to do and enjoy having the opportunity to choose their own activity and learning experiences.

Step 2

During this time, iron out the little things that stop children from being independent: not knowing where the pencils are; not knowing how to mop up spillage from the water tray; asking to go to the toilet. I often encourage teachers to keep a note of whenever they are interrupted for trivial things like this – and then plan how to eliminate the interruptions. While there are some younger children who still like coming up to show you things and share something with you, this is a moment's distraction compared to getting up and having to go to a stock cupboard. The aim is to be interrupted as little as possible – so that you are free to keep teaching or observing without distraction.

Step 3

Once the class is secure in its independence and you have made the necessary adjustments to where things are stored (see Chapter 6) or how things can be managed (have you mops and dustpans of the appropriate size, for example?), then you can introduce some adult-initiated activities (see Chapter 4) – activities where you put out resources with the intention that children learn something from your planning, but where you will leave them to be independent as learners. You then return later to see how they are getting on with the activity or resources and what they make of them. This will give you the opportunity to see whether the activities you plan are sufficiently open-ended to enable the children to be independent until *you* are ready to go to *them* (rather than them forming a queue to see you). It also shows the children that the classroom is a place where there will be a balance between learning that the adult initiates and learning that they initiate. Children are far more willing to tune in to the adult's requests if they know they have time to pursue their own interests in depth at a time not too far in the future.

My advice is that you include your TA in the 'becoming independent period'. We know that many unqualified staff – or staff without much experience or training for work with younger learners – do not always understand the need for independence. They want to 'help' and that help can take the form of 'doing it for them' – whether that be clearing up or drawing a flower. So, if our TAs are to be part of this learner-centred environment, then they must understand that the role of all adults is to support and not to 'rescue' children, to be there when needed but not to do things for them in order to speed things up.

> The role of all adults is to support and not to 'rescue' children.

Step 4

Once the classroom works smoothly *without you there*, then this is the time to introduce adult-focused learning. You and/or your TA can work with an individual or a group of children who need discrete adult time or where there are two or more children who need support on the same aspect of learning.

Adult-focused learning needs to be very carefully thought through. If you are teaching small groups rather than the whole class then you cannot cover everything with every group. This way of teaching is not like a merry-go-round of activities with everyone learning the same thing but just in smaller units. This would be exhausting and would not leave time for observation or for child-initiated learning.

If you are using a play-based approach to learning, then it is not necessary for all children to be taught the whole curriculum through adult-focused activities. Much of the Key Stage 1 curriculum can be learned through a well–planned environment for play and child-initiated experiences. The planning, of course, comes in the provision of resources and not in the learning outcomes (see Chapter 5 for a list of what is *not* likely to be learnt through play). So this leaves the teacher to decide which children need them most in order to achieve their 'next steps' of progress. Given that each teacher only has one pair of hands (and ears and eyes and one mouth), which group really needs the teacher to help them learn this new concept/skill (adult-focused activity) and who will learn it through a well-chosen adult-initiated activity? We know that children learn more securely

Adult-initiated learning can introduce children to the unexpected

when they try ideas out for themselves and when their experiences are active and first-hand. So a well-chosen adult-initiated activity will do perfectly well for some children, leaving the teacher free to focus on those children or those concepts that need more direct teaching at that moment.

Planning formats

As I said at the start of this chapter, I do not believe that planning formats matter – by that I mean that there is no 'right way' of planning. What matters is that the individual teacher has a way of capturing all the information they need to ensure that they are able to meet the learning needs of all the children in their class. How the teacher achieves this will be highly personal. Here are some case studies demonstrating three different strategies used by Key Stage 1 teachers to achieve the same purpose.

Case study 1

Teacher 1 has an A3 grid that is tied in to 'the triangle' (see Chapter 4). On the grid she plans for adult-focused activity and adult-initiated activity, and there is a blank column entitled 'child-initiated activity' where she writes down any resources or ideas she has to *extend* children's play beyond the continuous provision that is always available. The final column is also blank for observation and evaluation of all three kinds of activity.

Case study 2

Teacher 2 has an A4 sheet that identifies only what the adults will be doing. Her planning is, in fact, a timetable of adult-focused activity. So although, for example, from 9.00–10.00 the timetable says 'Phonics', that means that she and her TA will be leading small-group phonic teaching at that time (not the same group for the whole time though). It does *not* mean that the whole class will be doing phonics. The rest of the class are engaged in adult-initiated and child-initiated activity which is planned on another sheet. The children's independent learning does not stop and change at 10 a.m. (when the teacher's activity changes): rather, children move between adult-focused, adult-initiated and child-inaited activity seamlessly throughout the morning (see Chapter 4 and the section on 'Timetables' in this chapter).

Case study 3

Teacher 3 uses a 'day book'. In this A4 book she puts post-its and notes from her observations on the left-hand page and then her plans for the next day on the right-hand page. In this way, her observations are used regularly and planning is smack up to date and readjusted daily.

What all three teachers have in common is that their planning shows:

- *where* the planned activities will take place – i.e. indoors or outdoors;
- *where* the adult(s) will be for their adult-focused teaching.

All three teachers have prepared a 'rationale for continuous provision'. In other words, they have written down the 'potential learning' in water play, sand play, block play, etc. This does not change over time of course so, once written, it can be filed appropriately or, even better, displayed – with accompanying photographs – for parents and other visitors to see. In this way, teachers show that they know about the value of the continuous provision and can easily justify its place within the classroom.

Note that there is no *planning for play (other than extension resources (see e.g. Case Study 1) as play has no adult intentions or objectives and, if they are imposed, they change the activity to 'adult-initiated'.*

'Covering' the curriculum

Many Year 1 teachers continue to express concerns about 'covering the curriculum'. They find it hard to move from whole-class teaching that guarantees that all children have received the same teaching, to small-group work where different children received differentiated teaching.

In responding to this concern, the first issue to reiterate is that although all children are sitting on a carpet looking at a teacher, there is no guarantee that they are all learning what is on the teacher's plan. As pointed out earlier in this chapter, the chances of every child understanding, being interested in and tuning in to the teacher's learning objectives are remote. Whole-class teaching can only guarantee coverage of the curriculum, it cannot guarantee the learning of it.

> Whole-class teaching can only guarantee coverage of the curriculum, it cannot guarantee the learning of it.

Planning is far more effective when it offers children different learning opportunities, according to their current need. So, although all children might need to learn a certain skill or concept in time, some may learn it most effectively with an adult by their side and others may learn it by being engaged in more independent activities. Once something is introduced, some children may need additional reinforcement through an adult-focused activity and others may be able to transfer their learning immediately to an adult-initiated or even a child-initiated situation.

The point of small-group work is not to set up a carousel of activities whereby everyone gets the same teaching but just in smaller groups that rotate every so many minutes. If teachers fall back on this strategy then there are not many advantages over whole-class teaching. The point of a more flexible way of planning is to give children what they *need* – not necessarily to give them the same.

> The point of a more flexible way of planning is to give children what they *need* – not necessarily to give them the same.

Children's needs will change from day to day and the sensitive teacher, through her observations, comes to identify when one child might need more adult-focused time and another less. What this also means is that teaching objectives can be spread over more days. There is no need for every group to 'cover' the same objectives every day. One Year 1 teacher I know who adopted a more flexible way of working said that the biggest help for her was in seeing learning objectives across a week rather than across a day. In that way, the pressure to get round all children every day was alleviated and teaching became more relaxed.

What underpins this approach is a belief that through independent learning children learn, discover and consolidate a range of skills and concepts just as they do alongside an adult. However, even when teachers agree with this, they remain concerned that they may not 'see' all of the learning taking place when children are learning independently. That may indeed be true. Although play and independent learning need to be observed as rigorously as adult-focused learning, the teacher cannot be everywhere at once (which is the rationale for having more trained adults in the classroom). But does the fact that children are under the eye of an adult mean that their learning is more worthwhile? I do not think it does. When children are learning independently they learn a different range of skills then when they work alongside an adult. Therefore, high quality independent learning has value for children in its own right. But, in becoming confident about what is happening when she is *not* there, the teacher should have robust evidence from when she *is* there. When independent learning is observed, teachers should see children involved, engaged and learning in a range of successful ways. If this is the case when children are being observed, then the teacher can assume that this successful learning is also taking place when she is *not* there. For many teachers, once they have sufficient observations to feel their evidence is robust, then they feel more confident that this high quality independent learning is generally more valuable to the children than sitting on a carpet in a whole-class teaching situation.

'I would rather trust the children – and the learning environment I have created – than bring every child onto the carpet just so I can prove they have all heard the same thing.'

Sue: Year 1 teacher

'You cannot be everywhere and you *will* miss some learning nuggets, *but* even if all the children are on the carpet you will never know that they have all learned what you teach. That's why it's so important to observe independent learning to have evidence of the effectiveness of my planning of the environment and to see the peer learning that takes place.'

Pat: Year 1 teacher

Links between the Early Years Foundation Stage and Year 1

Finally we look at the links between the Early Years Foundation Stage curriculum and the National Curriculum for Key Stage 1. This is important not only because we want children's learning to flow smoothly from one key stage to the next, but because we know that most Year 1 teachers will be teaching both curricula in their Year 1 classes (see Chapter 2).

This should not be as daunting as it sounds. The way of working that is advocated in this book is concerned with *how* children learn rather than *what* they learn and, as such, whether planning for their learning needs is drawn from the EYFS or the National Curriculum is irrelevant. What matters is that teachers accommodate the natural, spontaneous learning styles and strategies of children who are 5, 6 and 7 years of age. As seen in Chapter 2, this means enabling children to be active, to be playful, to be independent, to be interactive and to follow their spontaneous interests. It means planning a careful programme of adult-initiated activities to bring about learning that is identified, through observation, as the next steps for individual children. It means adopting a developmental approach to teaching and not one that assumes that the Year 1 learning diet can or should be the same for every child.

In this time of change, when the Primary Curriculum is under review, teachers would do well to go back to the National Curriculum. If you look at the key concepts and skills that are laid down for Key Stage 1 learners, they are almost identical to those required of children at the end of the Foundation Stage. There is little that doesn't sit comfortably one with the other. The focus of teachers' attention should be on how that learning is organized and managed, and not what is contained in the learning objectives. In this way, both the Foundation Stage and the Key Stage 1 curriculum will appear to be a smooth and seamless learning experience for the children.

Conclusions

The overriding message of this chapter is to be flexible in your planning. No one knows your children's learning needs like you do and, armed with evidence gathered from your observations, you need the autonomy to plan learning experiences that are relevant, purposeful and meaningful to your class. Try not to get your planning as you want it and then fit the children into the plans. Rather, have the confidence to sort out the classroom management, the way the learning environment is organized, the children's independence and the observation of the children's learning – and then a system for planning that supports this way of learning and teaching can be developed over time.

Things to discuss in your school

- Is your short-term planning sufficiently flexible to respond to what you observe and assess each day?

- Does your planning show how children will learn independently as well as how they will learn when an adult is alongside them?

- Does your timetable currently interrupt children's learning too much? What can you do about this?

CHAPTER 9

The many different roles of the teacher

Introduction

As we alter our view of how children should learn, so we have to alter our view of what it means to be a teacher. Responding to the needs and interests of individual children places teachers in a different role to the person who dictates all the learning that takes place in the classroom.

The role we adopt as teachers is reflected in the learning environment we create, in the amount of choice and control we enable children to have and in the interactions we have with them. In a classroom planned for flexible learning the role of the adult must therefore be flexible. The adult will be – at different times – facilitator, interested observer, human resource, guide, expert and playmate. In a classroom that is committed to developmentally appropriate practice, the role of the teacher is to be what the child needs them to be.

> In a classroom that is committed to developmentally appropriate practice, the role of the teacher is to be what the child needs them to be.

Many of the different roles of the teacher have already been the subject of chapters of this book, but it is important to reiterate some of them here in order to see how they impact on one another.

Planning an appropriate learning environment

Whether a learning environment is 'appropriate' or not will depend on what a teacher is trying to achieve. If a teacher wants to encourage independent learning alongside high quality adult-led learning then the classroom environment must accommodate both these approaches.

As we saw in Chapter 6, the quality of the environment is what supports and sustains children's independence as learners, but this can lead teachers to question their role and ask, 'If the environment is so important, does this make me, as a teacher, less important?'

The answer to that question is emphatically 'No!': teachers are crucial because they create the environment. It is their insights, their observations of the children, their thoughts and reflections (and often their money) that create environments that support independent learning. So, teachers are incredibly important.

The good teacher, as we have seen, uses the planning and organization of the environment as a real-life learning opportunity for the children. There are myriad opportunities for children to plan, to problem-solve, to arrange, to evaluate their own learning spaces – both inside and out. It is the creative and confident teacher that passes such problem-solving and decision-making on to their class and encourages them to find workable solutions.

As has been said before, independent learning is not abandoned learning. While many of the children are working independently, the teacher will be either working with an adult-focused activity, or be observing or supporting more independent or child-initiated learning. The quality of the organization of the learning environment is what makes every element successful.

Knowing children well

Another critical role of the teacher is to know their children well. This may seem very obvious but it is worth emphasizing, in this context, why this is the case. Firstly, children are members of families and communities. What children bring with them to school is a reflection of their experiences when they are away from school. While some children are very forthcoming about what happens at home, and have positive stories that they want to tell, for others the home situation may be an unhappy or stressful one and one from which they want to escape when at school. For a teacher to be effective in their role they need to know all they can about the worlds in which their children are growing up. This knowledge cannot be gained through the child alone but needs to be learned from an ongoing relationship with parents and carers and through knowledge of the communities that are significant to children in their daily lives.

Parents and carers know things about the individual child that a teacher can never know. They take them to the shops, they tuck them into bed at night, they go away with them on holiday and they take them along to family gatherings. All the ordinary everyday experiences – and the special occasions – that make up the rich fabric of family life. The parent or carer will have very definite views about their child as a learner. They may be able to articulate these in the language of the school or they might need convincing that offering their account of an event over the weekend is valuable for the teacher to draw on as she plans for the child's next steps of learning.

The role of the teacher is to know children well for emotional and cognitive reasons. On a personal level it is about giving reassurance to the child and their family that they are safe, cared for and thought about especially. The EYFS promotes the 'key person' approach (see DCFS 2009: Card 2.4) to support this relationship. The key person is seen as the named member of staff who shows a 'special interest' in the child and 'holds the child in mind' when they are in the setting. They also maintain a close relationship with the child's family in order to ensure that the child is being 'appropriately cared for'.

But the role of the teacher goes beyond this social and emotional bond – crucial as it is, because knowing children well means being able to have the best starting points for children's future learning. It means being able to instigate learning conversations with them which stem from an intimate knowledge of their lives and interests away from home. How much easier it is to start a conversation with a child when you know about their experiences after school; when you can discuss their sick rabbit before expecting them to concentrate on their maths; when you can tune in to their current preoccupation with 'planets' in order to get across the concept of similarity and difference.

Knowing children well also entails knowing about and respecting the cultures and communities which impact on them as they live their daily lives: knowing whether a child goes straight from school to a prayer school to learn more about their family's faith; knowing whether certain food, celebrations or clothing are respectful or disrespectful to someone's culture; knowing that

High quality interactions are built on relaxed and playful relationships

a religious festival has deep significance to a family's and a community's activities at particular times in the year – all these things give teachers opportunities to relate to the child and their family and to use this knowledge to make learning relevant and meaningful to the child on a daily basis.

Modelling

It is always salutary to realize how important teachers are to young children. Most of us will have had parents or carers say that they have become fed up with hearing 'Miss X says this' or 'Mr Y told us it's like this' at home. We see children adopt our hairstyles, they comment on our clothes, and we hear – sometimes far too realistically – our words and turns of phrase being mimicked in the home corner. As significant adults in the lives of young children, we have to understand the influence we exert through all that we say and do. Given the esteem in which we are usually held, our actions and our words will be absorbed by osmosis and have a lasting impact on our children's development.

> As significant adults in the lives of young children we have to understand the influence we exert through all that we say and do.

Modelling behaviour

The first thing that we model is behaviour. If we want children to be respectful of others, then we must ensure that we show respect to them. If we want children to listen to each other then we must ensure that we listen to them. If we want children to be kind and thoughtful to others then we must be thoughtful about them. And it is not just our behaviour towards the children that matters – children will also pick up on our behaviour towards other adults. If relationships are curt or patronizing or sarcastic, then children may assume that this is an acceptable way of behaving and may one day emulate that behaviour themselves.

Modelling language

Teachers also model language. Alongside parents and carers we are in the important position of supporting children's language development as it becomes more sophisticated in its usage. But not only do we offer children correct grammar and appropriate and new vocabulary but, through language, we also convey powerful messages about our feelings, our ideas and our attitudes and we need to use our own language carefully if we want children to adopt a positive as well as accurate use of words and turns of phrase.

Modelling learning

Teachers need to model learning itself. This has two different elements. Firstly, children need to understand that as adults we go on learning and that learning doesn't stop when you leave school. An understanding of this is most likely to be achieved when an adult adopts the role of a 'co-learner' alongside the child, wanting to find out answers to questions to which neither knows the answer, or when the adult says 'Show me' to the child, in recognition that the child knows something that they do not. Such approaches send the message that 'not knowing' is only a stage in the process of 'coming to know', and that the important thing is not 'the knowing' but 'knowing how to find out'. This spirit of enquiry is one of the richest gifts that we can model for young children.

> The important thing is not 'the knowing' but 'knowing how to find out'.

Children need to come to understand that learning is something over which you have control as a human being, something at which you can get better. So, if a teacher says, 'I'm going to have to think really hard about that', or 'I can't remember, I'm thinking and thinking but it's gone out of my head', or 'I think if I write that down it will help me remember' – all of these strategies can reinforce the message that you can learn how to learn and can help your own learning to improve.

Tuning in to children

We know that much of children's learning depends on having the right starting point for consolidating or extending their thinking. A key role of the adult is to tune-in to what a child is currently thinking in order to build on and extend their understandings. We saw in Chapter 7 that the most effective way of tuning in to children's thinking is by observing them as they engage in the business of learning.

However, if observation is to be used as a strategy, then it must be given time, or adults can too easily make assumptions about what is preoccupying the child at that moment. It is all too easy, particularly when intervening in child-initiated activity, to jump in and start a conversation, only to find yourself greeted by a blank stare as children try and fathom why you have asked a question that bears no relation to what they were actually trying to do. Teachers need to stand back, watch and wait until they are clear about the child's line of enquiry.

> Teachers need to stand back and watch and wait until they are clear about the child's line of enquiry.

When adults watch children of this age, the children tend to do one of two things. Either they invite the adult into the activity – by showing them something or by sharing an idea with them or inviting them to take on a role, or they will ignore the adult because they do not need them at that particular time. Waiting to be 'invited in' is also an effective way of ensuring that the starting point for a learning conversation is coming from the child's current thinking rather than from the adult's preconceived ideas.

As well as observing children, adults need to listen to them. What children say is every bit as important in tuning-in to their current thinking as what children do. But listening to children is not just about hearing the words they speak, it is also showing that what they say has been heard – by the adult responding to and building on their ideas. Listening needs to be respectful. Only then will children feel more inclined to share their ideas and to offer suggestions and solutions without fear of saying the 'wrong' thing or their contribution being ignored.

When tuning-in to children, adults draw on their observations of children, their conversations with them and their knowledge of them: a complex mix of past and present evidence. Underpinning these observations and conversations is the body of teacher knowledge that is the foundation of our professional expertise: knowledge of child development – 'How would most children respond to this?'; 'What next step of learning would most children tend to take here?': and knowledge of curriculum development – 'What concept would best build on the child's current understanding of this aspect of maths or geography or creative development?'

Getting inside the mind of a child is very challenging, yet it is what teachers are doing every moment of every teaching day. We need to ensure that we give this complex task the time it needs in order to be sure that we know about the child's current thinking and do not presume.

Maintaining the learning momentum

If we acknowledge the driving force of children's own ideas, preoccupations and interests in planning for their learning then, having tuned-in to what these are, we need to ensure that we do not ignore them as we start talking to children about their activity and their thinking.

Very often, especially if teachers have initiated an activity, they begin to talk to children about it full of their own preconceived ideas concerning what should be happening and what children should be learning. Yet, as we have seen, unless an adult remains alongside an activity and steers and

Adults need to be alert to children's interests and lines of enquiry

guides it along their own pre-planned path, the chances are that children will take the activity down a path that is of interest to *them*, and not stay within the parameters that the teacher initially laid down. So, adults need to truly listen to what children are saying in order to hear the messages about learning that they are conveying. The skill lies in continuing a learning conversation based on what the child is saying rather than changing the direction of that conversation towards something that, from the adult's perspective, is deemed to be more worthwhile.

When we talk to other adults, we often find it easy to keep a genuine conversation going. Your friend says something and you respond; your sister says something and you ask a question to find out more. Yet, confronted by children, many adults find it hard to let the child's threads of thinking determine what is talked about. They feel compelled to put in a 'teacher question' to check up on whether the child has learned something they want them to learn, or change the direction of the conversation so that it leads more directly to an adult-determined outcome.

The skilful role of the adult is to follow the child's lead – to listen sufficiently respectfully to allow the child to steer the conversation; to respond to what the child says by asking genuine questions – not ones to which you already know the answer; to keep the conversation going so that your interest and your questions extend what the child is currently thinking and help them to see the world in new and different ways.

> The skilful role of the adult is to respond to what the child says by asking genuine questions – not ones to which you already know the answer.

The following are some transcripts of Year 1 children learning alongside adults. They show how easy it is for the adult to stop children's learning in its tracks rather than maintain the children's learning momentum.

Transcript 1

A group of Year 1 children are learning about materials. The children have been asked to find things in the classroom that have different textures.

Teacher:	How do you think the carpet feels?
Girl:	Cosy.
Teacher:	Cosy? Do you really?!
Girl:	*(pauses)* No.

Transcript 2

A Year 1 class have watched a DVD about people living in China. There follows a 'still' photo of a Chinese family.

Teacher: What do Chinese people look like?

No one answers other than one child who pulls their eyes so they slant

Teacher: Don't do that B. it's not a nice thing to do. Now come on the rest of you, what do Chinese people look like?

There is still no answer

Teacher:	Have you ever met Chinese people?
Boy:	Yes *(he names a child in the Year 2 class)*
Teacher:	And what do they look like?
Boy:	They look Chinese.

Transcript 3

A small group of Year 1 children are round the water tray experimenting with the boats they have built from different materials.

Child: I can see all kinds of reflections in this water.

Teacher: Good, but which of the boats is going to sink first do you think?

Child: Why does this reflection (pointing to one boat) move round like that?

Teacher: We'll worry about that once all the boats have sunk. Now, which one do you think is going to go under first?

Questioning children but not interrogating them

It can be very tempting to use questioning as the main way of eliciting children's thinking. But questioning children has its dangers. There are too many occasions when questioning interrogates children rather than illuminating their thinking.

> There are too many occasions when questioning interrogates children rather than illuminating their thinking.

Countless research articles have shown that questions are used by teachers to control children, to bring them back to the adult agenda, to limit the ideas that children have and, most of all, to check that children have learned what the teacher has taught them. None of these strategies are wrong in themselves, but if used to excess they perpetuate a classroom dominated by the teacher's agenda with little place for the children and their ideas. When the teacher asks most of the questions – most of which she knows the answer to – then children see questioning as something to 'get right', where there is one right answer – almost certainly already in the teacher's head.

Although there are occasions in life when we need to give an answer instantly, these are actually few and far between: when we go to the checkout and want to confirm that we have not been overcharged; when we are asked directions in the city centre; when answering in a test, exam or interview. But, in reality, most of the important questions of life, that have answers worth hearing, are those that take us time to answer. In fact, most of us know what it is like to be put under the stress of answering too quickly (say, in an interview) only to find, later in the day, that we can think of exactly what we should have said and could give a far better account of ourselves. Stress causes the brain to work less efficiently because it is too busy dealing with the stress to think about the issues at hand. So questioning that interrogates children – the quick-fire on-the-carpet-type of questioning – often produces the least efficient thinking.

Transcript 4

The teacher has set up an adult-initiated activity in the water tray. She has left funnels, pipes, pumps, cups and jugs in coloured water to encourage the children to explore the concept of capacity. The children have decided that they are going to make a milk-shake machine.

Teacher:	What's happening here?
Child 1:	We're making a magic milk-shake machine.
Teacher:	That's nice, but not what you're supposed to be doing! Did you find out how many of these cups filled that jug?
Child 2:	We're just putting the strawberry syrup in.
Teacher:	Yes, but how many cups filled that big jug? Did you try and find out?
Child 1:	Six.
Teacher:	How did you find that out?
Child 1:	No, it's nine, I forgot.
Teacher:	Shall we do it together?
Child 3:	*(Starts doing it very quickly)* Have we done it now?

'I even think that I was so focused on thinking up questions to extend the children that I wasn't really listening to what they were saying.'

Sara: Year 1 teacher

'I try to ask genuine questions and to watch and listen before I jump in. One of the most valuable lessons I learned was when a group of children were tearing up green paper towels and shredding them in the water tray. My initial reaction was one of anger until a child explained to me that this was in fact seaweed and they were creating an underwater world for the sea creatures I had set out. Had I been too quick to jump in, the creativity would have been lost!'

Sue: Year 1 teacher

The most important questions take time to answer. So in our Year 1 and Year 2 classes we should be concerned with asking the kind of questions that illuminate children's thinking, where children understand that there is more than one answer, where their answer has just as much validity as anyone else's, where they have a chance to go away and come back later with their thoughts after time for reflection. When a teacher really wants to come to understand what a child thinks or feels about something, then the child has to believe that their answer is worth waiting for. Here are some prompts that I use when I engage in conversations with children during their self-initiated learning.

Illuminating rather than interrogating children's thinking

- Don't ask questions to which you already know the answer (this has a place in the classroom but is basically 'checking up' on the child).

- Don't ask questions to which you do not want to know the answer (in other words, don't ask for a child's ideas if you have neither the time nor the inclination to follow them up).

- Don't ask questions to which you do not have time to wait for the answer (if you ask a question as you are 'walking by' then the child will not believe that you are interested in their answer and will not bother to give it thought. Teachers need to give children 'the time it takes' to reply).

- Don't ask questions that interrupt children's thinking (even 'What are you doing?' will cause a child who is deeply engaged in their learning to have to concentrate on you at that moment rather than on their learning).

- Don't ask too many questions (the best classrooms are those where children ask most of the questions, not the teacher).

Extending children's thinking

When adults come to extend children's thinking they draw – very often sub-consciously – on all of the information they have gleaned from watching, listening to and tuning in to children and their families over time. The more connected an adult can be with a child's current thinking the easier it is to use this knowledge and understanding to move the child's thinking on.

When adults are effective in extending children's thinking they have understood the child well enough and understand the potential learning well enough to know when to intervene and when not to, and to choose an intervention that will not detract from the child's current learning but enhance it.

Different adults use different strategies, but the following often bring about high quality thinking and learning in young children.

Strategies for extending children's thinking

The following list is not exhaustive. For some other ideas see Early Education's DVD material at www.early-education.org.uk.

Pondering
Asking a question to which you, the adult, do not know the answer. Posing it in such a way that the child believes you really do want to know. Posing it in a way that suggests you could 'find out together'. For example: 'I wonder what would happen if we remove that block now?' 'I wonder why those ants use that pathway to get down from the wall?'

Imagining
Through your comments and suggestions, taking the child to other alternative worlds. Drawing on their creativity to solve imaginary

problems or helping to put them into an imaginary situation. For example: 'When I came into school this morning I found these footprints. I think I need to tell the headteacher.' 'Now have you got everything we need for the pirates' invasion? It's too far to turn back once you set sail.'

Offering an alternative viewpoint

Reminding the child that others see the world differently, that their ideas and beliefs and feelings are not the only ones. For example: 'I wonder if Maggie would have thought the same thing?' 'I imagine that Noreen would have thought that was a cruel thing to do.'

Recapping

Going back over something with the child to show you have been paying attention. Offering them language to use that describes their own actions. For example: 'So you have been . . .'; 'So you think that . . .'

Thinking aloud

Saying aloud what you are thinking about and are going to try out for yourself, to give the child other ideas. For example: 'I think I'm going to add another section to this to make it stronger.' 'I really must organize what I'm doing for this afternoon so I think I'll make a list.'

Connecting

Placing the child's current learning in the context of what he has learned before and what he might learn in the future. For example: 'Do you remember when we tried to make the bulb light up, well . . .'; 'If you can manage to get this pole to balance then next time you might try . . .'

Explaining/informing

There are many occasions when a child needs to be told something – not everything all at once (not being taken off there and then to 'look in a book'), but a nugget of information that will just move them onto the next stage of thinking. For example: 'You can't make one the same because that is copyright and it's not allowed.' 'This is a piece of dowelling and it might hold those pieces together.'

Being silent

There are times when the best way to extend children's thinking is to say nothing – because the children are extending their thinking perfectly well on their own.

The role of the teacher in adult-focused, adult-initiated and child-initiated learning

We have seen that, in a learner-centred classroom, the role of the adult changes frequently. Choosing which role to adopt and when is a highly skilled business and teachers need considerable expertise to ensure they are extending children's thinking and not interfering with it. The most significant change in the adult's role comes perhaps when they move from initiating adult-led learning to supporting child-initiated learning. The following paragraphs explore this changing role and examine in particular the fluctuating control in learning outcomes between the adult and the child.

> Teachers need considerable expertise to ensure they are extending children's thinking and not interfering with it.

Adult-focused activity

When teachers are engaged in adult-focused teaching, then their role is clear. They have assessed the needs of their children, they have planned an appropriate activity or experience to give the children the 'next steps' in their learning and, as the teacher, they are there alongside the group to achieve the planned intentions.

The role of the adult in adult-focused activities

- Assess the needs of the children (prior to planning).
- Decide which child or children need to work with the teacher on a focused task.
- Stay with the child/children whilst the task is undertaken.
- Ensure planned learning outcomes are achieved.

Adult-initiated activity

In an adult-initiated activity, the adult's role changes, even though the adult has initiated the learning. This is because the adult will not stay with the child or children to control the learning that subsequently takes place. As a starting point, the teacher must have assessed the children's needs, of course, but here is where the similarity ends. The teacher will set up an activity or some resources in the learning environment (either indoors and or out) which she predicts will lead to learning that she feels is necessary or appropriate for a particular group of children or for the class as a whole. However, once the learning day is underway, the teacher will be working with an adult-focused group (or undertaking some observations) so, having introduced the adult-initiated activity, she will walk away from it and the children will learn independently. At an appropriate time during the session, the teacher will return to the group and observe and/or interact to see what has been learned. She will discover whether the activity was followed up in the way she had anticipated, or whether the children moved on to some other use for the resources, exploring some of their own ideas and interests. It may even be that the children have voted with their feet, and moved on to an entirely different child-initiated investigation.

The role of the adult in adult-initiated activities

- Assess the needs of the children (prior to planning the activity).

- Decide that the learning can be achieved independently.

- Plan a suitable open-ended activity.

- Set up the activity with the minimum of instructions and the maximum of open-ended possibilities.

- Return to the group, in due course, in order to show you have not abandoned them.

- Approach the group in a 'spirit of enquiry': I wonder what they made of this learning opportunity?

- Observe the learning at first and then, if appropriate, ask the children to explain or describe their learning.

Teachers often ask me whether I would select the children to undertake an adult-initiated activity or whether the activity is available as part of the general classroom provision for that day. The answer is – sometimes one and sometimes the other. Sometimes I might want certain children to engage in an activity, but feel I do not need or want to be alongside them as they learn, so I will start them off at that activity and return to my adult-focused group. Sometimes, I might want an activity to be available to all children and to see what they make of it (and indeed whether they go to it at all). So, like most things in the complex world of teaching, the adult has to use their professional judgement to decide what kind of activity will maximize their children's learning opportunities on any particular day.

Child-initiated activity

In child-initiated learning the role of the adult is different again. Here, the activity belongs far more to the children and so the adult must be careful not to interfere in the learning that takes place. The Oxfordshire Year 1 teachers found that, as the quality of play in their classes improved, the children seemed to need their intervention as teachers less and less. This may be for a number of reasons. Firstly, the role of the teacher is in creating the learning environment that will promote high quality play. So, much of the teacher's 'work' is done prior to the children arriving in the classroom. It is also the case that, by this age, many children do not need an adult as an 'audience' in the same way that 3- or 4-year-olds might. An adult is often seen as 'useful' – to hold something up high, to help manage something tricky, to fetch or find something handy – but often as little else. Also, by this age, children's play has become far more social and cooperative (see Broadhead 2004) and, therefore, the children's audience becomes each other rather than an adult.

However, children are endlessly different in their needs and wants, and the skill of the teacher is in being whatever the child needs you to be. So one child or group may want you to be an *interested observer*, there to see what is going on, but not to intervene. Some children may want you to be a *commentator*, to notice what they have done and to remark upon it and give it language. Some may want you to join in, to be a *co-player*, accepting the offer of the cup of tea or taking on the role of the mother, or seeing if you can build a car the same as theirs.

The role of the adult in child-initiated learning

- Be an *interested observer* – noting what is going on but not intervening.
- Be a *resource* – helping children or fetching things for them.
- Be a co-*player* – if children invite you in to their play (but don't impose your own objectives).
- Be a *commentator* – giving voice to children's emerging language and ideas.

'Time and again I have watched children abandon their play when I interrupt and I am beginning to realize I am only welcome when it is on their terms.'

Pat: Year 1 teacher

'When adults initiate activities they usually have to intervene more to sustain them.'

Nadia: Year 1 teacher

'I think children usually have greater perseverance when working on activities that they initiate by themselves, and then often I see my role as facilitator in providing additional resources or support.'

Sue: Year 1 teacher

'One of my firm beliefs is that as teachers we are far too quick to see a need and fill it. This is something I work very hard at, waiting for children to seek me out if they wish me to be involved in their play and not being too quick to jump in and help.'

Pat: Year 1 teacher

Conclusions

It seems to me that many of the current dilemmas faced by teachers in Key Stage 1 classrooms stem from an over-emphasis on *teaching* and a lack of attention to *learning.* Many teachers currently teaching in Key Stage 1 received an initial training that was concerned predominantly with the Literacy and Numeracy Strategies and too little time was given to encouraging an understanding of pedagogy in its widest sense or to teachers coming to hold their own beliefs about how children learn. The strategies often led student teachers to believe that if the instructions in the guidance manuals were followed then learning would take place. Unfortunately, learning is not so straightforward. Layered upon the intricacies of teaching a set of subject-specific skills are the individuality and idiosyncrasies of any given class of children. No one class is the same as another – even when they are in the same year group.

So, the roles of the adults in Key Stage 1 classrooms should be many and various. Every learning situation poses a different challenge and every child poses a different set of demands. Learning about the individual as well as the collective needs of a class will help teachers to be responsive to these various demands and to learn to be whatever the learning situation requires.

Things to discuss in your school

- How do you find out enough about the child, their family and their community to have the right starting points for learning?

- Who asks the most questions in your classroom?

- Does your teaching style change when you move from supporting adult-led to child-initiated learning?

Conclusions and reflections

As I said in the Introduction to this book, improving transition into Key Stage 1 is not straightforward. It involves adopting more developmentally appropriate practices and placing children back at the heart of pedagogy. It is not an easy option, but it is richly rewarding. When the curriculum draws on children's interests, it inevitably becomes more relevant and meaningful to them and, ultimately, more satisfying for their teachers.

If you are just beginning to introduce new ways of working with your Key Stage 1 children then be patient and remember that there will be setbacks before everything falls into place. I recommend that you find or establish a network of other Year 1 practitioners with whom to talk and compare practice. Get onto training courses about play, outdoor learning and supporting children's self-initiated activity. Above all, keep involving all those in your own school – particularly those with management responsibility – so that they support your efforts and increasingly come to understand just what you are aiming to achieve.

At the end of the Oxfordshire Transition Project and at the conclusion of training courses on transition, I ask practitioners what would be the one message they would pass on to teachers who are about to begin the journey towards a more balanced approach to learning and teaching in Key Stage 1. The answers that I most frequently receive are below. While in each case I have used the words of individuals, these represent the responses from countless teachers who have made the journey on which you are about to embark. From all of us: good luck!

'Play only gets to be of high quality when it is given long extended periods of time.'

'Don't underestimate the importance of the classroom environment. I never realized how much my tables and chairs were determining the children's learning experiences – and how boring and repetitive these were!'

'Persevere! You will doubt yourself and doubt whether this works, but it does. You just have to "get it". For me, the key was not neglecting the play but getting in there and really watching and understanding exactly what the children were learning.'

'Just wait for the impact this has on your children – my children are now happy, really involved in their learning and don't need to be nagged at to finish work.'

'Get your TAs involved. They can really help – and they can really get in the way if they don't understand child-initiated learning!'

'My biggest word of advice? Stop focusing on the paperwork and maximize time to be with and tune-in to the children!'

'This is the most empowered I have ever felt as a teacher. If you want creativity and inspiration back in your job . . . then teach this way.'

'Look at experiences from the children's perspective. This course has made me realize that the 5- and 6-year-olds in our school get completely different learning experiences according to whether they are in the R/1 class or the 1/2 class. This shouldn't be the case when they are the same age children.'

'The minute my head understood what I was doing I was away. He's completely on board now and it's made such a difference in terms of expectations and resourcing.'

'Child-initiated learning improves behaviour! I didn't believe it until I'd tried it for a few weeks. But all those children that struggle to sit still and concentrate have shown me they can concentrate – on their own learning. So now I can plan things I know will engage them in different ways and not give them all the same curriculum experience.'

'Make best friends with the Foundation Stage staff. They are the experts in the school and I am learning more from them all the time.'

'The less I speak the more I hear the "voice" of the child. I am better now at responding individually to the child with English as an additional language, the quiet child and especially the child who doesn't appear interested (but really is – but in his own way).'

'Really ask yourself how children learn, and then keep that at the heart of all you do.'

References

Alexander, R. (2009) *Towards a New Primary Curriculum: A Report from the Cambridge Primary Review. Part 2: The Future.* Cambridge: University of Cambridge.

Bandura, A. (1977) *Social Learning Theory.* Upper Saddle River, NJ: Prentice Hall.

Bilton, H. (2002) *Outdoor Play in the Early Years: Management and Innovation*, 2nd edn. London: David Fulton.

Bredekamp, S. (ed.) (1987) *Developmentally Appropriate Practice in Early Childhood Programs Serving Children from Birth through Age 8.* Washington, DC: NAEYC.

Broadhead, P. (2004) *Early Years Play and Learning: Developing Social Skills and Cooperation.* London: RoutledgeFalmer.

Bruce, T. (1991) *Time to Play in Early Childhood Education.* London: Hodder & Stoughton.

Claxton, G. (1997) *Hare Brain, Tortoise Mind: Why intelligence Increases When You Think Less.* London: Fourth Estate.

Council for the Curriculum, Examinations and Assessment (2007) *The Revised Curriculum.* Belfast: CCEA.

DCELLS (Department for Children, Education, Lifelong Learning and Skills) (2008) *Framework for Children's Learning for 3–7-year-olds in Wales.* Cardiff: Welsh Assembly.

DCSF (Department for Children, Schools and Families) (2008) *The Early Years Foundation Stage.* Nottingham: DfES Publications.

DCSF (Department for Children, Schools and Families) (2009) *The Independent Review of the Primary Curriculum: Final Report.* Nottingham: DCSF Publications.

DfEE (Department for Education and Employment) (1998) *The National Literacy Strategy.* Suffolk: DfEE Publications.

DfEE (Department for Education and Employment) (1999) *The National Numeracy Strategy.* Suffolk: DfEE Publications.

DfES (Department for Education and Skills) (2000) *Curriculum Guidance for the Foundation Stage.* Nottingham: DfES Publications.

DfES (Department for Education and Skills) (2003) *Excellence and Enjoyment: A Strategy for Primary Schools.* Nottingham: DfES Publications.

Donaldson, M. (1978) *Children's Minds.* London: Fontana.

Dweck, C. (1978) Children's interpretation of evaluative feedback: the effect of social cues on learned helplessness, *Merrill Palmer Quarterly,* 22(2).

Edgington, M. (2004) *The Foundation Stage Teacher in Action,* 3rd edn. London: Paul Chapman.

Elley, W.B. (1992) *How in the World do Students Read? IEA Study of Reading Literacy.* The Hague: IEA.

Fisher, J. (2008) *Starting from the Child,* 3rd edn. Maidenhead: Open University Press.

Fisher, J. (2009) 'We used to play in Foundation, it was more funner': investigating feelings about transition from Foundation Stage to Year 1, *Early Years,* 29(2): 131–45.

Fromberg, D.P. and Bergen, D. (2006) *Play from Birth to Twelve: Contexts, Perspectives and Meanings,* 2nd edn. Abingdon: Routledge.

Holditch, L. (1992) *Understanding Your 5 Year-Old.* London: Rosendale Press.

Hughes, F.P. (2009) *Children, Play and Development,* 4th edn. London: Sage.

Lindon, J. (1993) *Child Development from Birth to Eight: A Practical Focus.* London: National Children's Bureau.

Moyles, J. (1993) *Just Playing? The Role and Status of Play in Early Childhood Education,* 2nd edn. Buckingham: Open University Press.

NAA (National Assessment Agency) (2005) *Continuing the Learning Journey.* London: QCA.

OCC (Oxfordshire County Council) (2006) *Transition: Foundation Stage to Year One.* Oxford: OCC Early Years Team.

OCC (Oxfordshire County Council) (2009) *Transition: Building on Foundation Stage Practice in Year One.* Oxford: OCC Early Years Team.

Ofsted (Office for Standards in Education) (2004) *Transition from the Reception Year Year 1: An Evaluation by HMI.* London: Ofsted.

Osborne, E. (1997) *Understanding Your 7-year-old.* London: Rosendale Press.

Piaget, J. (1952) *The Child's Conception of Number.* London: Routledge & Kegan Paul.

Piaget, J. and Inhelder, B. (1969) *The Psychology of the Child.* New York: Basic Books.

Robinson, M. (2008) *Child Development from Birth to Eight.* Maidenhead: Open University Press.

Sanders, D., White, G., Burge, B. *et al.* (2005) *A Study of the Transition from the Foundation Stage to Key Stage 1.* DfES Research report SSU/2005/FR/013. London: DfES.

Scottish Executive (2008) *Curriculum for Excellence.* Edinburgh: Scottish Executive.

Sharp, C. (1998) Age of starting school and the early years curriculum, Paper prepared for the NFER Annual Conference, NFER, Slough, October.

Sharp, C. (2002) School starting age: European policy and recent research, Paper presented at the Local Government Association seminar, NFER, Slough, November.

Sharp, C. and Hutchinson, D. (1997) *How Do Season of Birth and Length of School Affect Children's Attainment at Key Stage 1? A Question Revisited.* Slough: NFER.

Siraj-Blatchford, I., Sylva, K., Laugharne, J., Milton, E. and Charles, F. (2006) *The Monitoring and Evaluation of the Implementation of the Foundation Phase Project across Wales.* London: Institute of Education.

Steiner, D. (1993) *Understanding Your 6-year-old.* London: Rosendale Press.

Tassoni, P. (2007) *Child Development 6 to 16 Years.* Oxford: Heinemann.

Tymms, P., Merrell, C. and Henderson, B. (1997) The first year at school: a quantitative investigation of the attainment and progress of pupils, *Educational Research and Evaluation,* 3(2): 101–18.

Tymms, P., Merrell, C. and Henderson, B. (2000) Baseline assessment and progress during the first three years at school, *Educational Research and Evaluation,* 6(2): 105–29.

White, J. (2008) *Playing and Learning Outdoors.* London: Routledge.

Wood, E. and Attfield, J. (2005) *Play, Learning and the Early Childhood Curriculum,* 2nd edn. London: Paul Chapman.

Woodhead, M. (1989) 'School starts at five . . . or four years old': the rationale for changing admissions policies in England and Wales, *Journal of Education Policy,* 4(1): 1–21.

Index

Locators shown in *italics* refer to boxes, case studies, pictorial illustrations.

Related books from Open University Press

Purchase from www.openup.co.uk or order through your local bookseller

STARTING FROM THE CHILD 3e

Julie Fisher

- How can early years practitioners build on children's competence and autonomy as effective early learners?
- How do adults get to know children sufficiently well to plan effectively for their learning needs?
- How can early years practitioners plan for high quality child-initiated experiences alongside more focused adult-initiated learning?

Early years practitioners continue to face the dilemma of planning for the needs of individual children whilst meeting the demands of targets and goals set by government. In such a pressurized climate, it can be all too easy to go with what is imposed, rather than stand up for what young children need and are entitled to.

In a practical and realistic way, the third edition of *Starting from the Child* supports practitioners in the Foundation Stage to be advocates for young children and their learning needs. Julie Fisher outlines the important theories and research which should underpin decisions about best practice. She offers meaningful and inspirational ways of developing appropriate learning environments and experiences for Foundation Stage children.

Revised and updated throughout, the new edition includes:

- Latest research impacting on our understanding of early learning
- Reference to recent government initiatives such as the Early Years Foundation Stage
- An extended explanation of how to plan for child-initiated learning alongside adult-initiated learning
- A completely revised chapter on 'The place of play', with a new focus on different types and contexts for play, cultural influences and the role of the adult in supporting play
- Two new chapters on the observation and assessment of children's learning, and self-evaluation for practitioners

Starting from the Child is essential reading, not only for early years practitioners, but for all those who manage and make decisions about early learning.

Contents

List of boxes and figures – Preface to the Third Edition – Acknowledgements – Competent young learners: What children know and can do – Conversations and observations: Learning about individual children – Planning for learning: Decisions about appropriate experiences to support and extend learning – The role of the adult: Making the best use of teaching time – Encouraging independence: Environments that develop children's learning autonomy – Collaboration and cooperation: The importance of talking and learning with others – The place of play: The status of child-initiated experiences – The negotiated learning environment: Issues of ownership, power and control – The assessment of children's learning: What practitioners need to know about their children and their achievements – Reflection and evaluation: What practitioners need to know about their practice, their provision and themselves – References – Index.

2007   240pp   978–0–335–22384–8 (Paperback)

EARLY YEARS FOUNDATIONS
MEETING THE CHALLENGE

Janet Moyles

With so many challenges facing early years professionals, there are continual dilemmas arising between doing what one knows is essentially 'right' for birth-to-five-year-olds from all backgrounds and conforming to the demands made by government and policy makers. This exciting and original book supports practitioners in thinking through their roles to meet some of the many issues they encounter.

Using the new *Early Years Foundation Stage* principles as its framework, the contributors support early years professionals in dealing with issues and challenges in a sensitive and professional manner, with particular emphasis upon the need for practitioners to personalise the requirements for each child in their care and to reflect closely upon their own and children's experiences.

The writers are all experienced and avid early years advocates. Their topics include: the changing landscape of early childhood, culture, identity and diversity, supporting playful learning, outdoor learning, documenting children's experiences, developing independence in learning, the meaning of being creative, play and mark-making in maths, and literacy.

Each section is introduced with some background research and information to provide evidence and guidance upon which practitioners can make their own decisions. Individual chapters include questions for reflection, points for discussion and suggestions for additional reading.

Early Years Foundations: Meeting the Challenge is essential reading for the full range of practitioners working and playing with birth-to-five-year-olds.

Contributors
Deborah Albon, Pat Broadhead, Liz Brooker, Naima Browne, Elizabeth Carruthers, Tricia David, Dan Davies, Jackie Eyles, Hilary Fabian, Rose Griffiths, Alan Howe, Paulette Luff, Rod Parker-Rees, Theodora Papatheodorou, Emmie Short, David Whitebread, Marian Whitehead and Maulfry Worthington.

Contents
Notes on contributors – Introduction – Changing the landscape of early childhood – Section one: A unique child – Introduction – Primary communication: What can adults learn from babies? – Difference, culture and diversity: Challenges, responsibilities and opportunities – Identity and children as learners – Section two: Positive relationships – Introduction – Working together to support playful learning and transition – Somebody else's business: A parent's view of childhood – Coping with bereavement – Vision, mission, method: Challenges and issues in developing the role of the early years mentor teacher – Birth-to-three: The need for a loving and educated workforce – Section three: Enabling Environments – Introduction – The challenges of starting school – Children's outdoor experiences: A sense of adventure? – Written observations or walks in the park? Documenting children's experience – Food for thought: The importance of food and eating in early childhood practice – Section four: Learning and development – Introduction – Developing independence in learning – What does it mean to be creative? – Multi-modality, play and children's mark-making in maths – 'Hi Granny! I'm writing a novel.' Literacy in early childhood: Joys, issues and challenges – Endpiece – Appendix – Index.

2007   308pp   978–0–335–22349–7 (Paperback)   978–0–335–22348–0 (Hardback)

IMPLEMENTING THE EARLY YEARS FOUNDATION STAGE
A HANDBOOK

Pat Beckley; Karen Elvidge; Helen Hendry

- Are you working or training to work in the early years sector?
- Would you like support and guidance in understanding the key themes in the Early Years Foundation Stage document?
- Are you looking for practical tips and strategies on how to implement EYFS in your setting?

Yes? Then this is the essential guide for you!

Relating the themes from the EYFS document to everyday practice can be a daunting prospect for the busy practitioner. This timely resource offers friendly advice and suggestions on how you can apply the document's strategies to your own setting.

Through practical activities and case studies, the authors provide you with straight forward guidelines for implementing the statutory requirements and developing your practice. The book covers the main outline of the document, providing a discussion for the themes and rational as well as making links to current research, theory and practice.

Each chapter includes:

- An introduction to the theme
- Practical suggestions and activities
- Reflective tasks
- Case studies of good practice

This book is essential reading for anyone involved with the early years sector whether you are a student, practitioner, childminder or parent.

Contents

Introduction – Child development – Inclusive practice – Keeping safe – Health and wellbeing – Respecting each other – Parents as partners – Supporting learning – Key person – Observation, assessment and planning Supporting every child – The learning environment – The wider context / multi-agency collaboration – Play and exploration – Active learning – Creativity and critical thinking – The welfare requirements – Personal, social and emotional development – Communication, language and literacy – Problem solving, reasoning and numeracy – Knowledge and understanding of the world – Creative development – Physical development – Conclusions – Further reflections – Appendices – Index – Glossary

2009   280pp   978–0–335–23615–2 (Paperback)   978–0–335–23616–9 (Hardback)